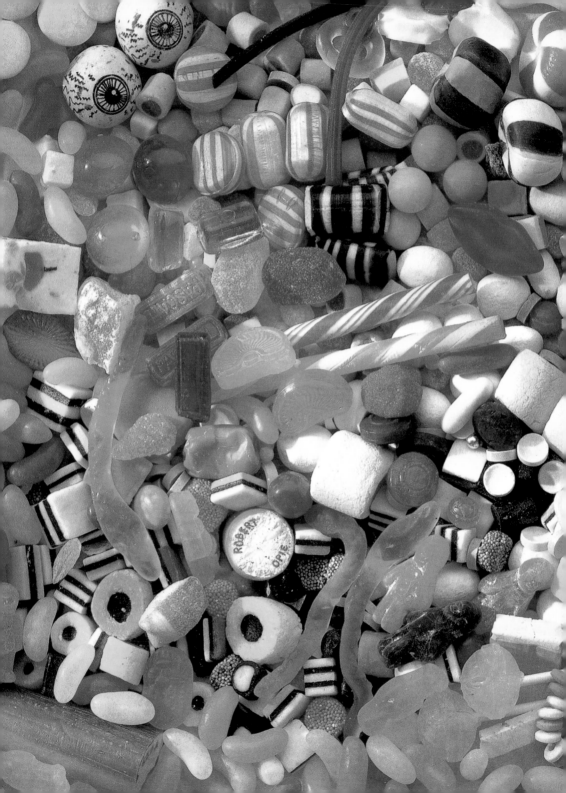

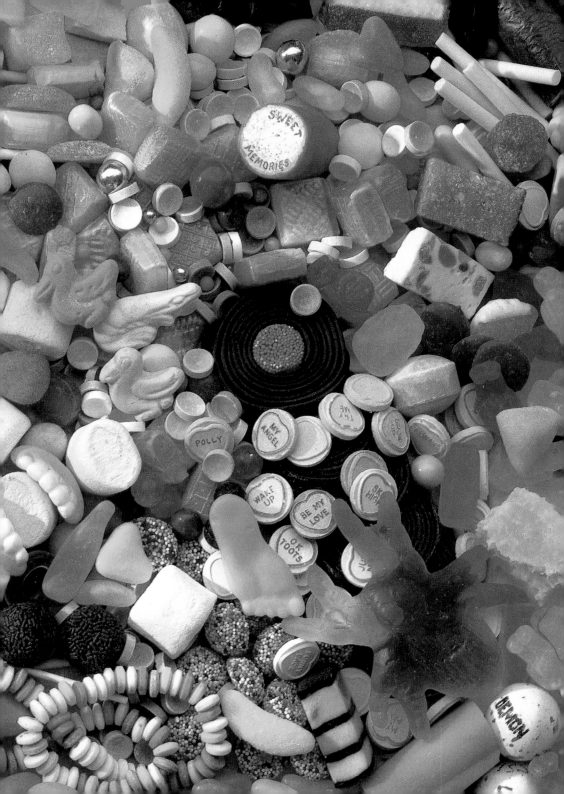

ROBERT OPIE
Sweet
Memories

PAVILION

ROBERT OPIE
Sweet
Memories

A SELECTION OF CONFECTIONERY DELIGHTS

SAMPLED BY ROBERT OPIE

A sweet-toothed family: Robert Opie (on the right) aged 8.

This edition published in Great Britain in 1999 by
PAVILION BOOKS LIMITED
London House, Great Eastern Wharf
Parkgate Road, London SW11 4NQ

First published in 1988 by Pavilion Books Limited

Copyright © Robert Opie 1988,1999

Design and layout © Pavilion Books Ltd.

The moral right of the author
has been asserted

A CIP catalogue record for this book is available
from the British Library.

ISBN 1 86205 309 X

Printed in Singapore by Kyodo

2 4 6 8 10 9 7 5 3 1

This book can be ordered direct from the publisher. Please contact
the Marketing Department. But try your bookshop first.

CONTENTS

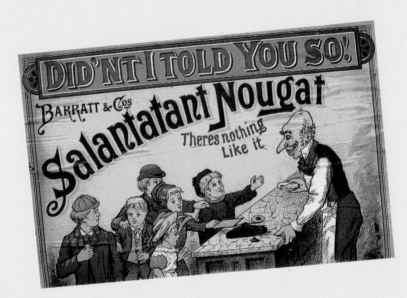

FOREWORD

Thomas Edison once said that genius was one per cent inspiration and ninety-nine per cent perspiration. Genius apart, my quota of inspiration came one Sunday twenty-five years ago, on 8 September 1963. I was in Inverness, mid-journey from Edinburgh to the very north of Scotland, when the pangs of hunger prompted me to find something to eat. My search ended with the purchase of a pack of Mackintosh's Munchies and a pack of McVitie's Ginger Nut biscuits, both from a vending machine as there were no shops open on a Sunday afternoon. It suddenly dawned on me, while consuming the Munchies, that when I threw the Munchies pack away, I would also be throwing away a small fragment of history.

Furthermore, the thought occurred to me that if I was to save the wrappers, tins and bottles from every product I bought, collectively they would represent a social history of life in Britain. I knew from my childhood experience of collecting Lesney 'Matchbox' miniature die-cast toys and from my research into philatelic postal stationery, that there was continual change. Pack designs would be updated, new products would arrive, others disappear, and the advertisements for the products would tell of other aspects of social change. From that moment on I was to keep everything – for better or for worse.

I was sixteen when I had this vision and, looking back on it, I can only surmise that my thoughts must have been provoked by the previous ten days. I had spent them with my parents at meetings held in Aberdeen by the British Association for the Advancement of Science where my father was President of the Anthropological Section. My mind was obviously in overdrive.

Collecting packaging was eventually going to take up a lot of space, and soon I realized the need not only for somewhere to display the everyday things of our throw-away lives, but also for somewhere to store them. The idea of a museum became stronger when, a few years later, I started to research and gather examples of earlier packs and advertisements relating to the origins of Britain's hundred year old 'pack age'.

In 1984, with 250,000 items to house, a museum was finally established and set up in a Victorian warehouse in the docks at Gloucester. This is the Museum of Advertising and Packaging and also the fruits of my 99 per cent perspiration. This is not the end though of either the inspiration or the perspiration, as this particular centre for the artifacts of our consumer society now needs to expand.

However, it has already proved to be a place where you can not only follow the social changes of a nation, but also experience the most nostalgic feelings. Jogged by the wrappers and advertisements of yesteryear, memories come back of such delights as the gob-stopper, dyed in layers of bright colours – purple, pink, poison green: 'You took the gob-stopper out of your mouth at intervals, sometimes in order to speak and sometimes to see what colour it had now become.' There are memories of the fourteen bulls-eyes that could be bought for a farthing and having to extract the last sticky one from the corner of the paper bag; memories of the jelly babies that were bitten into head first, and the fruit gums that were so useful as jewels on the crowns in the nativity play. Memories of action sweets such as sherbet fountains, sugar whistles and those lemon sherbets from which the fizz could be sucked. Memories of the brands that have disappeared – Fry's Five Boys, Rowntree's Motoring Chocolate and Mars' Spangles, and memories of Russian Toffee, 'black as ebony and nearly as hard', and said to be a more civilized way of extracting milk teeth than tying one end of a thread round the wobbly tooth and the other to a door knob.

No book can hope to recapture fully these forgotten moments, but perhaps the images here will succeed in conjuring up some sweet memories.

Fry's showcard, c.1930.

INTRODUCTION

Today, whether we like them or not, sweets can play a far more important role than simply that of nourishing food. More than just a quick source of energy, a snack, or a sweet sensation they can be a reward, a comfort, an enticement, a token of appreciation or even an object for barter at school.

An example of their role can be seen in the way that sweets – and chocolates in particular – have become above anything else a vital part of the language of love. This association appears to go back many centuries. When knights were bold, sugar confections were costly, though worth the expense to sweeten the breath before approaching a pretty maiden. Shakespeare describes some sugary delights as 'kissing-comfits' in *The Merry Wives of Windsor* when Falstaff declares:

'Let the sky rain potatoes,
Let it thunder to the tune of Greensleeves,
Hail kissing-comfits, and snow eringoes.'

(The eringoes mentioned were the candied roots of the sea-holly and were considered to be an aphrodisiac.)

In time, the manufacturers of sweetmeats (as sweet confections were called in the seventeenth century) promoted the love interest, calling their products by various names including sweetheart cachous, sugar kisses and cupid's whispers. Conversation lozenges were introduced with romantic messages inscribed on them such as 'Meet me by moonlight' and 'Forget me not'. Today's Love Hearts made by Swizzle Matlow have been around for over fifty years and still bear similar mottoes.

Since then luxurious chocolates have been developed with soft centres, nut fillings and exotic cremes. Packed in substantial decorative boxes, these delights have taken over as the suitor's standard offering. Many would have us believe that it is an essential part of courtship: 'and all because the lady loves . . .'

It is not surprising that with the natural human craving for sweetness confectionery becomes an addiction for many people. Even so, it has only been during the last hundred years that chocolates and sugar confections have become cheap enough for the addiction to take hold (a similar development to that of cigarette smoking).

The British sweet tooth has sunk deep into the economy – over £3000 million is spent on chocolates, toffees, boiled sweets and bars every year. During a sunny bank holiday weekend, four million sticks of rock are sold at over three hundred seaside resorts, each one with the town's name running right through the middle of it from one end to the other; a feat of confectionery engineering that has puzzled many a child – and the occasional adult.

Display box label, c.1885.

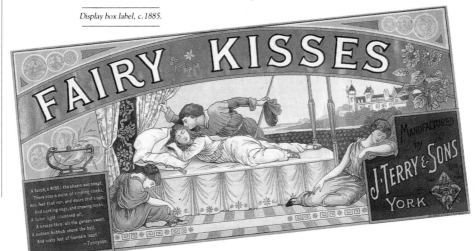

A DIP INTO HISTORY

It is not popularly appreciated that the variety and range of sweets on offer today has become available only during the last hundred years. Many of today's leading brands are, in fact, less than sixty years old. Crunchie was launched in 1929, Mars Bar in 1932, Black Magic in 1933 and both Kit Kat and Quality Street in 1937. Conversely, younger generations do not always realize for how long such brands have been part of people's lives.

The origins of confectionery can be traced back to about 2000BC when the ancient Egyptians satisfied their cravings for something sweet by combining fruits and nuts with honey. Liquorice juice, extracted from the root of the leguminous 'Sweet Root', is known to have been used for medicinal purposes at about the same time. The forerunner of today's Turkish delight was an unpromising confection of boiled grape juice and starch cut into squares. Over 3000 years ago the Aztecs in Mexico were known to use the cocoa bean to make a bitter drink. However, it took 1500 years before that drink could be sweetened with sugar.

SUGAR

Sugar cane appears to have been indigenous to India, and 2000 years ago sugar confections of some kind were being made there. The growing of sugar cane spread to Egypt and China and it was not long before sugar became a merchantable commodity. By the sixth century the Arabs were growing sugar cane and two hundred years later it is recorded as having reached Sicily. The Crusaders apparently returned to their native homes bearing sugar. Venetian merchants started to trade in it and the first major consignment arrived in London in 1319.

During the Middle Ages, however, sugar was costly, being measured by the ounce and afforded only by the wealthiest. At this time, it was the apothecaries who made the best use of sugar: by mixing it with their potions it tempered the taste of their medicines, giving rise to the phrase, 'sweetening the pill'. Sugar was thought to have healing properties, a factor which undoubtedly helped the

Display box label, c. 1895.

sale of their medicines, but the apothecaries also found a ready market for sugar confections in their own right – for those who could afford them. In France sugared almonds became popular and in Italy *confetti* (small, hard, sugar plums) were eaten especially on celebratory occasions.

The cultivation of sugar cane was introduced into the West Indies by Christopher Columbus in 1493, and the English first established cane plantations on Barbados in 1657. However, it was not until 1747 that a German scientist succeeded in extracting sugar from beet, although it was the French who perfected the process in 1812. By 1880 beet had become the main source of sugar for Europe.

COCOA AND CHOCOLATE

It was the combination of sugar and cocoa that eventually set the confectionery story alight. The Spanish conqueror of Mexico, Cortez, brought cocoa and the chocolate drink back to Spain in 1502. The addition of sugar made this bitter drink more palatable, but it took almost another hundred years for the new drink to reach the rest of Europe.

The first shop to sell drinking chocolate in London was opened in 1657 and, in time, many chocolate-drinking houses opened, such as Whites and the Cocoa Tree, some of which developed into men's clubs. In his inimitable way, Samuel Pepys described his first taste of the chocolate drink. He

ABOVE *Fry's Cocoa label, c. 1830.*
OPPOSITE *Suchard poster, c. 1895.*

records in his diary for 24 November 1664, 'Up and to the office, where all the morning busy answering of people. About noon out with Comissioner Pett, and he and I to a Coffee-house to drink jocolatte, very good.' By the end of the seventeenth century, milk was being added to the drink, and in rare instances chocolate was being eaten.

In 1728, Walter Churchman set up shop in Bristol. He was highly successful in the making of drinking chocolate and was granted Letters Patent, a licence, by George II a year later. In 1761 Dr Joseph Fry, a Quaker physician with wide scientific interests, purchased Churchman's shop. From these early beginnings the processing of cocoa grew slowly until 1795 when Fry's installed one of the first steam engines in their factory to grind the cocoa beans.

At this time there were many small businesses trying their hand at making sugar confections. These early enterprises were usually no more than individuals supplying local needs, and often making the sweets along with other foodstuffs. For

Chocolate wrappers in the late Victorian style: Peter's was withdrawn in the 1960s; Lindt, who have produced chocolate since 1845, still use the same wrapper today.

those who succeeded in finding a satisfactory recipe or an ability to market their produce better than others, business would prosper. One such firm was that of Berry and Bayldon who had made confectionery since 1767. In 1828 they were joined by Joseph Terry who was instrumental in laying the foundations of the famous company.

Whereas the eighteenth century was witness to the birth of some prominent confectionery manufacturers, it was the nineteenth century that saw their rapid expansion. The advance in mechanization coupled with other benefits of the Industrial Revolution, such as improved distribution, ensured their growth.

John Cadbury opened a shop in 1824 in Birmingham selling tea, coffee and cocoa; his cocoa manufacturing business started a few years later. During the 1840s both Fry's and Cadbury's were producing chocolate made specifically for eating, although the vast majority of production was geared towards the manufacture of cocoa.

The popularity of cocoa and chocolate was limited to the wealthy until 1853 when Gladstone greatly reduced the import duty tax. Along with improvements based on continental recipes, the cheaper products quite naturally stimulated demand. It was also in 1853 that Fry's launched their chocolate cream sticks, the forerunners of Chocolate Cream Bars, thus helping to combat French imports.

In 1862, Henry Rowntree acquired the cocoa and chocolate business of William Tuke & Sons, a firm founded in York by a Quaker woman, Mary Tuke, in the early eighteenth century. Seventeen years later Rowntree's began to manufacture pastilles and gums, products which had previously been the monopoly of the French.

THE CONTINENTAL FIRMS

During the nineteenth century there was much activity in Europe where chocolate works were opening and expanding. In 1819 François-Louis Cailler founded the first Swiss chocolate factory near Vevey, (he had worked in the Caffarel chocolate factory in Milan for four years prior to that date), and in 1825 Philippe Suchard started his confectioner's business in Neuchâtel, France. A few years later Charles-Amédée Köhler started to

Trade card, c.1900.

produce chocolate in Lausanne, Switzerland; in one of his many experiments he invented hazelnut chocolate.

It was the Swiss who made the final and most significant breakthrough in the chocolate story. In 1875 Daniel Peter made a milk chocolate for eating by adding condensed milk, the creation of his neighbour Henri Nestlé.

Another well-known name was that of Jean Tobler. He had sold chocolate specialities, many of his own making, since 1868 when he had set up shop in Berne. His chocolate sold so well that he found it necessary to start manufacture on a bigger scale, and by the end of the century was exporting to Britain. The famous Toblerone three-cornered pack containing the Swiss Alpine milk chocolate with almonds and honey arrived at the turn of the century. The distinctive mountain range shape is possibly the only chocolate mould to have ever been patented, and when this was done in Switzerland the authorizing signature was that of Albert Einstein, who happened to be working in the Patent Office at the time.

Considering Peter's success with the tastier milk chocolate, it is surprising that it was over twenty years before any British firms manufactured it. Cadbury's were the first when they launched their Milk Chocolate in 1897.

Cadbury's Dairy Milk display box label, in use from 1905 until the 1920s.

CHOCOLATE BARS

Following the success of the Fry's Chocolate Cream Bar launched in 1866 (remoulded in 1875 into the shape it remains today), other chocolate bars were produced, being sold unwrapped from 'outer' boxes made of wood. It was later in the century that the more expensive bars were individually wrapped. This was the case with the first two milk chocolate bars. Fry's Milk Chocolate was launched in 1902, and employed a most endearing image on its wrapper – the faces of five boys showing the transformation of expression when being consoled with Fry's chocolate. This popular image had been used since 1886 to advertise Fry's.

A sweeter chocolate came in 1905 with Cadbury's Dairy Milk, and there followed a succession of milk chocolate bars with various ingredients, such as Nut Milk in 1907, Fruit & Nut in 1921 and Brazil Nut in 1925. Cadbury's Neopolitan arrived in 1908 and two years later Bournville Plain Chocolate. The need for sustaining chocolate bars during the First World War increased their popularity.

Early Fry's and Cadbury's chocolate boxes from the 1880s and 1890s.

CHOCOLATE BOXES

During the second half of the nineteenth century certain types of chocolate were being sold in decorative boxes. As early as 1861 Cadbury's mentioned 'fancy boxes' in its price list. The boxes were used for such delights as Extra Superfine Chocolate Creams. In 1867 Cadbury's *Chocolat des Delices aux Fruits* could be bought in a fancy box, as well as loose. In 1868 both Fry's and Cadbury's offered decorative printed chocolate boxes for the Christmas market and then the Easter trade. The range of pictorial designs soon became vast. In 1882, for example, Rowntree's offered no less than 150 different sentimental pictures during a single season, with prices ranging from 4d to 2/6d.

Eventually, by the late 1890s, most firms had standard ranges of boxed chocolates and Terry's in particular specialized in this area of the confectionery market. Cadbury's 'King George V' chocolates, launched in 1911 for his coronation, became the key assortment to which every manufacturer aspired. Then in 1914 Cadbury's released their Plain Tray assortment and Milk Tray followed a year later. Originally sold loose from trays, the 'box for the pocket' was available by 1916. Priced for the cheaper end of the market, the boxed Milk Tray proved extremely popular even though they were rather more expensive than buying the chocolates loose.

During the 1920s the boxes for most chocolates were quite substantial, and it was not until the 1930s that a more economic box was used for brands like Terry's All Gold (1932) and, after extensive research, Rowntree's Black Magic (1933). In 1936 Rowntree's launched Dairy Box as a direct competitor to Cadbury's Milk Tray; in the same year Mackintosh introduced a mixture of chocolates and toffees called Quality Street, followed two years later by Cadbury's Roses.

OTHER TYPES OF CONFECTIONERY

Along with the innumerable sugar confections – suckers, quenchers, humbugs, fudge and nougat – there was the flexible liquorice. An early manufacturer of liquorice was George Dunhill who devised the Pontefract cake in 1760. Liquorice has been particularly popular with children who delight in the many forms it can take – liquorice telephones, skipping ropes, wrist watches and firemen's hoses.

The poor man's sweet, the toffee, was beginning to make its mark in Britain in the nineteenth century. Having come originally from Turkey, toffee slowly established a place in the market, with the first major factory for caramel toffee being founded in 1883. In 1890 John Mackintosh blended the traditional brittle English toffee with the soft American caramel to sell in his shop in Halifax. He called it Mackintosh's Celebrated Toffee and in 1899 a large factory had to be built to accommodate the rapid rise in sales.

It was not until the First World War that the firm of Edward Sharp expanded rapidly from their factory in Maidstone, Kent, where they had been in business since 1878. By the 1920s the character of Sir Kreemy Knut was familiar to everyone since he continually appeared in advertisements and on the sides of the orange-coloured Sharp's tins of Super Kreem Toffee, often accompanied by a parrot. In 1923 Sharp's launched Home-made Super Kreem, selling it in shaped Kreemy Kottage tins along with their other novelty tins of seaside buckets and toy drums.

MEDICINAL CONFECTIONERY

From the Middle Ages sugar has been mixed with medicines to make them more palatable. Parkinsons of Burnley, for example, claimed that they sold more sugar coated pills than any other firm in the world. From the beginning of the twentieth century there were many lozenges, gums and pastilles that served as throat soothers, tummy

Souvenir card given by F. Allen & Sons at the International Health Exhibition, 1884.

Display card, c. 1930.

warmers or healthy energy givers. The products that fulfilled these roles were those like Zubes (Hoarse? Go Suck a Zube), Hacks and Tunes; Victory V Gums were advertised as good for cold journeys, as were Lofthouse's Fisherman's Friend and Boyle's Linseed Licorice & Chlorodyne – 'warms yer inside'; for energy, Trebor Barley Sugar sticks (contains pure medicinal glucose 'life's vital force') and Nurse Grant's lemon barley sugar tablets containing healthy glucose. An extension to throat lozenges were voice ju-jubes developed for the benefit of actors, singers and public speakers.

CHEWING GUM

The ancient Greeks, as ever, chewed gum, making it from the base of the mastic tree. Grecian women found it cleaned their teeth and sweetened their breath. Modern gum is made with chicle, the juice of the spodilla tree grown in South America, and was being chewed by Americans in the 1860s. Vending machines were developed particularly for chewing gum, and in the United States from 1888 Tutti Frutti Gum was first sold from vending machines.

In 1892 William Wrigley started to sell chewing gum in Chicago. His first brands were Lotta Gum and Vassar. Juicy Fruit and Spearmint followed in the next year. In 1911 Wrigley's chewing gum arrived in Britain, mainly being sold from vending machines. It was Wrigley's who invented the handy opener tape in 1932. At this time chewing gum was recommended after meals or smoking to cleanse the mouth, to aid digestion, to sweeten the breath and to keep teeth healthy.

CONFECTIONERY IN THE TWENTIETH CENTURY

The price of chocolate rose steadily during the First World War, but after 1921 prices fell during the decade and, as a result, sales increased. Between 1924 and 1939 the consumption of confectionery per head rose by over 50 per cent, yet expenditure per head declined by 13 per cent. In August 1938, for instance, Cadbury's announced that during the previous month they had brought prices down and were now giving more chocolate for the money – a 2oz bar of Fruit and Nut now cost 2d.

Besides the attention given to the manufacture of boxed chocolates, a whole new range of chocolate bars were made available. Rowntree's Motoring Chocolate was introduced in 1926, Fry's Crunchie in 1929 and Cadbury's Whole Nut in 1933.

In 1932 Forrest Mars arrived in Britain from the United States and started to produce the famous Mars Bar from his factory in Slough. Milky Way followed in 1935 (already launched in the United States as early as 1923). A year later, Maltesers – tiny pieces of Horlicks-flavoured dough exploded in a vacuum and coated in chocolate – were launched. Rowntree's Aero (it looked good value because the bubbles increased the visual size of the bar) was introduced in 1935 at the same time as Chocolate Crisp, which was to be renamed as Kit Kat two years later. Also in 1937 came Rowntree's Rolo and Smarties (a new name for their chocolate beans). Perhaps the most immediate sensation at the time was the introduction of Nestlé's Milky Bar because the 'chocolate' was white.

By 1938 some 300,000 shops were selling sweets in Britain, and they were supplied by 350 confectionery manufacturers. At this time, an average of 7oz of sweets per week was consumed by each person in the United Kingdom whereas in the United States the figure was 4½oz. But all this was to change with the outbreak of the Second World War. Sweets were rationed for over ten years, from July 1942 until the much awaited 4 February 1953, just in time for the coronation of Elizabeth II.

Shortages of materials during the War and the immediate post-War period led to adaptations in the ingredients of sweets. Most notable of these was the need to introduce blended chocolate, which contained a proportion of separated milk, since full-cream milk was not available.

Few successful product launches were made, or attempted, during this period of austerity, but in 1948 two brands appeared. One was Rowntree's Polo Mints – the mint with the hole. The idea had been captured from the American GIs who sucked a product called Lifesavers (the American for life belts). The other launch was from Mars: suckable boiled sweets in a tube called Spangles.

On 22 September 1955 commercial television started transmitting the first commercial break which included an advertisement for Murraymints, 'the too-good-to-hurry mints'. Another of the early TV slogans was that for Rowntree's Fruit Gums: 'Don't forget the Fruit Gums, Mum'.

From now on, not only were the jingles on everyone's lips, but a hefty proportion of confectionery advertising expenditure was switched to this powerful voice, touting for business in the very homes of sweet lovers throughout the country. The Milky Bar Kid, for example, has become legendary, having appeared on television since 1961.

The fifties and sixties were a period of rationalization for the confectionery industry. Beecham's bought Pascall in 1959 and then sold them ten years later to Cadbury's along with Murray's. In the early 1950s Guinness bought two confectionery companies, Callard & Bowser and Riley's Toffee. In the 1960s the Barker & Dobson group acquired the toffee firm of Benson and the long-established company Fryer, makers of the renowned Victory-V gums and lozenges since the late 1880s. Fox's Glacier Mints were acquired by Mackintosh in 1969 who, in turn, merged with Rowntree's in the same year.

The Mars Group made their mark at this time with a series of brand launches, including Bounty in 1951, Galaxy in 1958 and in 1967 both Twix and Marathon. Mackintosh's introduced a number of boxed varieties – Week-End (1957), Good News (1960) and Reward (1965). Fry's brought out Picnic in 1958, and Cadbury's entered Contrast into the market in 1962 as a plain assortment, later to be relaunched with both milk and plain chocolates. The major triumph of Rowntree's during this period was After Eight, introduced in 1962.

In the 1970s Mars, Cadbury's and Rowntree's marketed forty-four new brands between them. Most of them failed including Aztec, Amazin Raisin and Rumba. Old Jamaica and Ice Breaker, both manufactured by Cadbury's, were among the withdrawn brands, but recently they have been re-introduced. One success for Cadbury's has been the development of a two-layered chocolate bar, consisting of a soft nougatine layer and a crisp layer of crushed cereals. Appropriately named Double Decker, this new combination of tastes has been on sale since 1977.

However, a major upset to Cadbury's dominance in the chocolate slab market came in 1976 when Rowntree's devised a chunky chocolate bar called Yorkie. At this time the traditional Cadbury bars had become gradually thinner and the bite sensation had all but disappeared. Yorkie capitalized on its chunkiness and the rugged image associated with truck drivers. In response, Cadbury's re-launched their Dairy Milk bars using a chunky mould in 1978.

Confectionery has developed rapidly in the last hundred years, to the extent that today the country consumes 600 million Mars Bars every year, 200 million Cadbury's Creme Eggs and enough Kit Kats to keep pace with a machine that produces 80,000 bars an hour.

Display card, c.1955.

ADVERTISING AND PROMOTION

Harry Lauder tin, c. 1910.

There must have been great excitement one morning when an employee of the Anglo-French Confectionery Company opened a letter congratulating them on their toffee. Not an unusual event, but then this particular letter had come from the great music hall star, Sir Harry Lauder. It read:

> My Dear Sirs,
> Your Toffee is perfection, or as I ought to say,
> Your Confection is Perfection.
> Yours sincerely
> Harry Lauder.

Such an excellent testimonial could hardly be kept a secret. Having gained the cooperation of Sir Harry, the Company decided to adapt their tins by depicting this splendid letter along with an illustration of Harry Lauder. Unfortunately it is not recorded how well this association helped sales.

For those companies without the good fortune of such spontaneous patronage, an approach to the right person could still be tried. One firm that did this was C.T. & W. Holloway who in the 1890s gained the support of the opera prima donna, Adelina Patti. She even agreed, for a consideration, to allow the company's Voice Confectionery to be branded Pattines, adding that she was 'much pleased' with the voice lozenges.

In the 1920s and 1930s it became necessary for the many toffee manufacturers to distinguish their products from all the others. When a firm could not

Pattines tin, c. 1895.

afford massive advertising, they had to rely on the more immediate appearance of the product. Thus splendid and glamorous tins abounded with bright colours and decorative patterns. The use of a tin also enhanced the status of the toffees or boiled sweets inside, making them a more acceptable gift in comparison with the prestigious box of chocolates.

But a better promotion was to associate the product with an existing and much-loved character or film star. Thus Mickey Mouse Toffee, Felix Cream Toffee, Tiger Tim Toffee, Jackie Coogan's Cream Toffee and Kinema Toffee with Charlie Chaplin's face on the side all appeared on sweet shop shelves. In the nineteenth century, too, manufacturers had made free use of famous people's names to distinguish their sugar concoctions, such as Bonaparte's Ribs and Nelson's Bullets.

However, the majority of firms relied on the natural appeal of the product itself, enhanced by the names given to the tasty morsels – Batger's Buttered Brazils, Lett's Pineapple Chunks, Toyplane Toffee, Benson's Super Cream Hydro Toffee or Mackintosh's Egg & Cream Toffee de Luxe. Along with each enticing name, the manufacturer dreamt up some short description or 'puff'. Many centred on their products being wholesome, delicious and nutritious; for example both Nestlé and Mackintosh used the phrase 'overflowing with goodness'. Pascall's summed up their description of Ambrosia Devonshire Chocolate as 'the glory of Devon in a packet', and their Cuties as 'sugared sunshine'.

It is interesting to note how seventy years ago so many confectionery items emphasized the quality. Thus for Halton's Honey & Milk Toffee (packed in a beehive-shaped tin) there is a statement on the base saying, 'You may with safety give your children Halton's Toffees and Tablets. Their absolute purity is guaranteed, combining as they do a wholesome food-sweet and a most delicious Confection.'

The art of giving intriguing names to confectionery lines was foremost amongst the firms who specialized in sweets for children. The leading exponent of alluring titles was Barratt's with, to name but a few, Laughing Irish Eyes (eight for a 1d), Hippopotamus Eyes, Ogo-Pogo Eyes, Jumping Japs, and the optimistically named Ever-

Price cards, c.1935.

lasting Strip (two for a 1d). Barratt's did not have the monopoly on enticing names, and other firms produced Black Jacks, Chocolate Banana Fingers, Umbrella Lollies and Tom Thumb Drops, and everyone could create favourites like Pink and White Sugar Mice. Another favourite was the Lucky or Mystery bag. The lucky dip element of these bags lured many a child into buying them, even though the bags always contained a similar selection of small confections and a cheap novelty.

Nestlé's wrapper, 1930s.

The association between royal events and confectionery began in earnest with the celebrations for the coronation of Edward VII in 1902. Manufacturers produced boxes and tins containing boiled sweets and chocolates to commemorate the event. The tins especially were highly decorative and, for subsequent coronations, jubilees, royal visits to cities and exhibitions, the souvenir commemorative tin became part of the celebration. For the Wembley Empire Exhibition of 1924 many of the toffee firms, including Sharp, Mackintosh, Riley and Thorne, issued tins depicting Exhibition scenes. Again at Wembley, some forty years later Lovells, a toffee firm, issued a tin in the shape of a football for the 1966 World Cup.

During the first forty years of this century sweet companies developed many exciting taste sensations in order to promote eating chocolate. These often used combinations of chocolate with fruits, nuts, caramel, marzipan, toffee, peppermint, nougat, truffles and wafers. Furthermore the bite was affected by how the chocolate was moulded: a thick bar of chocolate has quite a different feel to that of a thin chocolate cat's tongue; above all, bubble-filled chocolate such as Aero has a totally different taste from a crumbly Cadbury's Flake; the size of a mouth-stretching Mars Bar is smiles apart from a chocolate croquette (a disc-like tablet). Since then, the variations have been endless, not to mention the many that have been tested but never reached the shops.

By the end of the nineteenth century the more realistic ideals of marketing had given rise to brand names that focussed on particular occasions when sweets could be eaten. These included Bensdorp's After Five Chocolates (After Eight did not arrive till 1962), Edmondson's Cruising Toffees, Walter's Riverside Assortment and the recently introduced Hallowe'en Pack by Barratt's. Perhaps the award for targeting a market goes to Nestlé's who produced Smokers' Semi-sweet Milk Chocolate in about 1930, said to be 'specially blended to suit smokers. It is just sweet enough, very sustaining, and does not create thirst. You will find it particularly pleasant between smokes.'

Confectionery has always been promoted as a source of energy, being sustaining and nourishing. No wonder that explorers like Nansen and Scott loaded their sledges with chocolate. Soldiers needed sustenance as well, and some products alluded to this. Needler's Military Mints were credited with the patronage of the forces during the Great War – 'they are sustaining and refreshing, and the mint gives a slight feeling of warmth.' The United Confectionery Company developed the aptly named 'Marchatese' Mints – 'thirst quenching for the military, specially prepared for all persons engaged in fatiguing duties.' For the home front, Cadbury's created Excursion Chocolate and Holiday Chocolate which contained almonds and raisins – a bar which had previously been promoted as a hiking snack. Rowntree's Motoring Chocolate also contained almonds and raisins and, as the name implied, was promoted as the chocolate to stash away in the glove compartment, in the same way as Yorkie is today. A press advertisement for 1926 sums up the feeling: 'For the jolly days of Easter it's a happy idea to take Cadbury's Chocolate on your adventures. On walks a ½lb block keeps you going, and it's just as handy when motoring.' In those days the pace of motoring was slower, more of an expedition than a race, with a greater chance of being stranded.

During the 1920s it was becoming common for people to have leisure time at the weekend and, with the popularity of motor cars, this was when they could get away from it all. The result was a proliferation of weekend assortments from the confectionery firms keen to cash in on the new trend.

Tins from the years 1915–20.

However, for the confectionery trade, the most important times to encourage the sale of tins of sweets and large exotic boxes of chocolates were Christmas and Easter. Before Christmas each manufacturer issued a catalogue of their special ranges which would be available to entice the public; by the 1920s this included Christmas selection boxes which would contain samples of the company's most popular lines. Some of the largest would have held up to sixteen different brands. In many instances the boxes themselves had games or puzzles printed on them.

Commemoratives: Queen Victoria's Jubilee, 1897 (Callard & Bowser); Edward VII's Coronation, 1902 (Fry's and Rowntree's); George V's Coronation, 1911 (Faulder's and Fry's); Princess Mary's wedding, 1922 (Sharp's); Wembley Empire Exhibition, 1924 (Rowntree's and Mackintosh); George V's Silver Jubilee, 1935 (Fry's); Edward VIII's intended Coronation, 1936 (Caley's); George VI's Coronation, 1937 (Cadbury's); Festival of Britain, 1951 (Nestlé's); Elizabeth II's Coronation 1953 (Rowntree's Aero and Kit Kat).

Holiday Chocolate, launched in 1929.

By the 1930s sweets were being stuffed into almost any household object – Rowntree's offered a chromium teapot ('note the special ebonite heat-resisting base') filled with chocolates for 5/6d, a little cheaper was Nestlé's 5/– Royal Winton teapot packed with choice chocolates, ('beautiful as a show-piece this lovely teapot will also prove a most serviceable addition to your tea-table'.) Fry's offered everything from a brass coal scuttle filled with chocolate bars and boxes for 21/–, to a glass pickle jar with fork for 2/6d. But it was Needlers who in 1936 found the gift 'you simply cannot do without'. It was the Knitcraft case for 5/–, a 'useful and attractive container for your work, wool, needles, etc.' and containing 4/– worth of County Chocolates.

Throughout the last hundred years, the sale of confectionery has continually increased (the rationing years excepted), and expenditure on advertising has kept pace. In the 1880s the chocolate

Rowntree's 5/– Selection box, 1939,
including Smarties and Kit Kat.

firms concentrated on the sale of cocoa and drinking chocolate. But as sweets became more tasty and more popular, more attention was given to promoting them. One of the early advertisements given national coverage was that for Fry's Chocolate showing the appealing image of five boys. This classic advertisement first appeared in 1886 and enamel signs and showcards displayed the image in streets and shops for years to come.

The arrival of Fry's Milk Chocolate and Cadbury's Dairy Milk at the turn of the century stimulated the promotion of chocolate for eating. By now the cost of chocolate had become sufficiently low for most people to be able to afford it. It was around this time that the selling of boxed chocolates became increasingly important and, as sales of cocoa for drinking had now reached a peak, manufacturers increasingly concentrated on devising new chocolate brands and publicizing them.

In the 1930s there were as many as sixty prominent advertisers of confectionery. The main promotional expenditure went on hoarding posters, display cards for the shops and advertisements in the newspapers and magazines. Manufacturers were

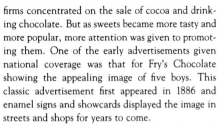

Christmas over-wrappers, c. 1930.

Tins of 'Week-end' sweets, depicting the latest roadster to give the purchaser that get-away-from-it-all feeling. The Maynard's tin, c. 1925, suggested that it was 'well worth taking home'. Maynard opened his first shop in 1876; there were some 100 outlets operating by early this century. Maynards were the originators of the wine gum which arrived in 1909. Walters' Palm Week-end Tin was available around 1930.

quick to realize that the effect of advertising could be remarkable. In the case of Fox's Glacier Mints (a brand originally distributed only in the Midlands), within two years of beginning national advertising in 1920 the output from their factory at Leicester had to increase six times.

During the 1950s and after, many changes took place in the retailing and marketing of sweets. The arrival of the self-service supermarket created a new style of shopping, and slowly the grocers began to take sales away from the independent sweet shops (by 1971 a third of confectionery sales went through grocers). In 1955 commercial television started, so much of the advertising budget swung to the small screen. As it happened there was a gradual movement for confectioners and news-agents to become self-service, and this in turn meant that during the sixties and seventies the traditional shop window disappeared, and thus the need to supply vast quantities of point-of-sale display material.

A further reason for the success of the grocery trade was the abolition of retail price maintenance on confectionery in the early 1960s. This enabled cut-price sweets to be sold and cleared the way for the selling of multipacks. One of the first was Kit Kat in 1963, selling six two-finger bars cellophane wrapped together. Within five years 20 per cent of Kit Kat sales were accounted for by the multipack. Another development was the introduction of miniature 'fun-size' bars, a quantity being sold to-gether in a single bag. They were popular in the United States, and in 1972 Mars promoted the idea in Britain.

During the last thirty years there has been a greater emphasis placed on the use of slogans with-in the confectionery market. Many of these have been popularized through the use of television commercials. For instance, 'Have a break, have a Kit Kat' has been used since 1959, and 'A Mars a day helps you work, rest and play' for a similar time. The advertising theme with probably the longest life of all is Cadbury's image of a glass and a half of milk in every bar, which has now been in use for sixty years.

Apart from the extensive use of promotions linked to money-off vouchers or self-liquidating offers there have been many consumer competitions, especially during the 1960s. Michael Miles, the host for TV's popular 'Take Your Pick' show, was involved in one for Cadbury's Lucky Numbers sweets when the prize was a night out in London. Also in 1965, Cadbury's ran a competition where the entrants hoped to win free chocolates every day for a year. A particularly successful promotion was that for Cadbury's Dairy Milk which captured the philanthropic spirit of the early Quakers. The pub-lic were encouraged to nominate someone who 'for a simple everyday act of kindness, cheerfulness or courtesy' would be presented with a C.D.M. (Cadbury's Dairy Milk) award which comprised a casket containing a presentation scroll, a C.D.M. award ribbon plus a ½lb bar of chocolate.

LEFT *Card replicas of Rowntree's gift caskets, c. 1905–11. By the end of the nineteenth century, manufacturers had discovered the housewife's enjoyment of collecting gift coupons given away with the products she bought. In the case of cocoa manufacturers, especially Rowntree's and Cadbury's, coupons from cocoa packs could be saved up to be exchanged for a highly decorative tin filled with chocolates or other sweets. Rowntree's in particular, found this form of promotion successful and continued using coupons until the late 1930s, by which time a full range of gifts was available, from bars of chocolate to cutlery and silk stockings. Customers often expressed their delight at the decorative tins; typical is this example from 1911: 'I beg to thank you for beautiful Coronation Casket received safely . . . It surpassed all my expectations. It is a perfect gem and reflects the greatest credit on the designer.'*

ABOVE *Barker & Dobson's Television Selection, early 1950s: something to chew while watching the box. In the 1920s, the firm of Kenyon introduced their Radio Toffee: the brand 'to listen with'.*

RIGHT *Fry's display card, c. 1930. The collecting instinct was exploited by many manufacturers, notably the cigarette companies, who introduced small illustrated cards into their packs. Issued in series of flowers, animals, monarchs and so on, once the set had been completed, it could be mounted in a special album, such as that produced for Fry's. Also during the 1930s, Nestlé's gave a small happy families game card with each 1d bar. Once collected, the set of 48 could be exchanged for a full-size pack, 'free of advertisement'.*

ABOVE RIGHT *Cadbury's display card to promote the CDM Award, 1965.*

*Caley's Easter egg box label, drawn by
John Hassall. The orange character is
Ruff-and-Ready, the hero of The Magic
Shop by May Byron, published in 1905.*

Easter egg display cards, c. 1930. A popular theme was for Easter chicks to take on human endeavours. The first hollow chocolate Easter eggs were produced by Fry's and Cadbury's in the mid-1870s, sometimes filled with sweets. By the 1890s eggs were being covered individually by wicker, later by moulded card with a decorative print and then in solid square boxes. Cadbury's had introduced their creme eggs by the 1920s and in the 1930s Easter novelties reached a peak, when the chocolate was covered with intricate patterns of sugar or marzipan. Eggs were sold with free gifts such as flower vases or toys, (for example a pull-along quacking duck). The idea of using a card case with holes on each side was the inspiration of a designer experimenting with light bulb cartons. In the 1950s manufacturers began packing Easter eggs in this way, since when the art of card origami has become surprisingly intricate.

ABOVE *Christmas selection boxes by
Rowntree's, late 1920s.*

OPPOSITE *Cadbury's Christmas club savings
posters, c. 1935.*
*The biggest season in the confectionery
calendar was, and still is, the Christmas
period. Every year for the past century,
(except in the 1940s), sweet firms have
produced catalogues, proudly displaying their
latest novelties and boxes. Selection boxes
have been sold since Edwardian days, with
names such as Christmas Parcel (Batger's),
Xmas Tuck Box (Caley's) and Xmas Gift
Box (Needler's, established in 1886), but it
was not until the 1920s that they became an
established part of the festive scene.*

A CENTURY OF IMAGES

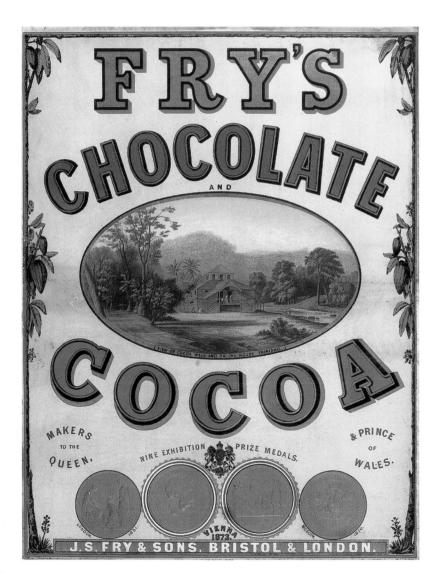

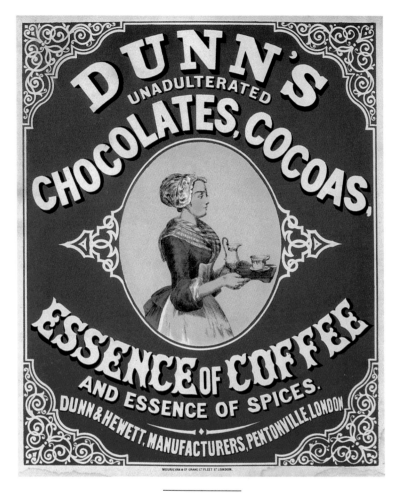

ABOVE *Dunn's showcard, c. 1880.*

OPPOSITE *Fry's showcard, c. 1875, which could refer to both chocolate for eating and chocolate for drinking; drinking chocolate was more common at this time. Regular international exhibitions began in the 1850s, at which medals were awarded for excellence. Fry's, for example, were awarded a gold medal in Vienna in 1873 and in Paris in 1878 (where Dunn & Hewett received two silver medals). By 1900, Fry's had accumulated over 300 medals and diplomas from such exhibitions.*

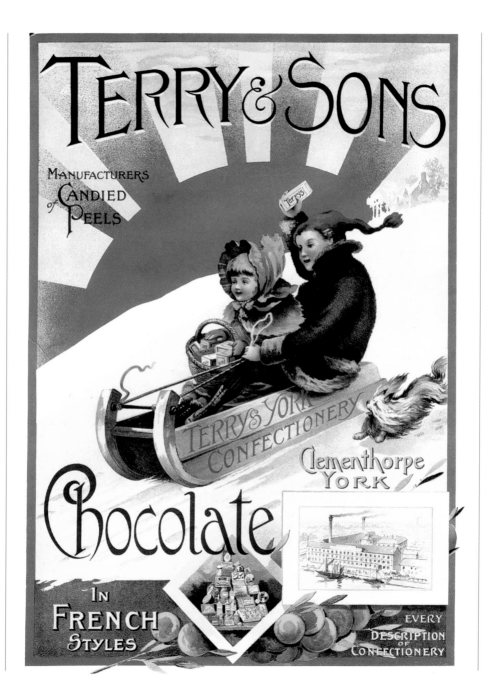

ABOVE *Callard & Bowser showcard, c.1890. The girl holds open an outer box of individually wrapped packs of butterscotch. The other well-known manufacturer of butterscotch was Parkinson's of Doncaster who originally set up business as a family grocer in 1817.*

OPPOSITE *Terry's showcard, c.1880. To describe chocolate as 'In French Style' was the pinnacle of good taste. Terry's were among the first companies to introduce eating chocolate in the 1880s and pioneered boxed chocolate assortments at the beginning of this century.*

ABOVE *Mackintosh's showcard from the late 1890s. Sent to an Eton schoolboy, this tin proudly displays Queen Victoria's coat of arms.*

OPPOSITE *Keiller's showcard, c. 1895. James Keiller first sold marmalade in 1797 and, to many manufacturers of preserves, using sugar to make sweets as well must have seemed a natural progression.*

ABOVE *Fry's advertisements, c. 1900, drawn by Tom Brown.*

OPPOSITE *Fry's advertisement, c.1895. These illustrations show scenes of the children's 'Aladdin's cave'. Confections can be seen in their display boxes on the counter-top.*

ABOVE *Callard & Bowser butterscotch tins, late 1890s. These highly decorative tins were produced for children who could use them as attractive containers when they were empty.*

OPPOSITE *Caley's showcard, c. 1905. The firm of A.J. Caley became well-known for three quite different commodities: mineral water, chocolate, and crackers. Caley began as a chemist, introducing mineral waters in the 1870s. In 1883 the firm started manufacturing cocoa, developing into the making of chocolate three years later. In 1898 they began producing crackers.*

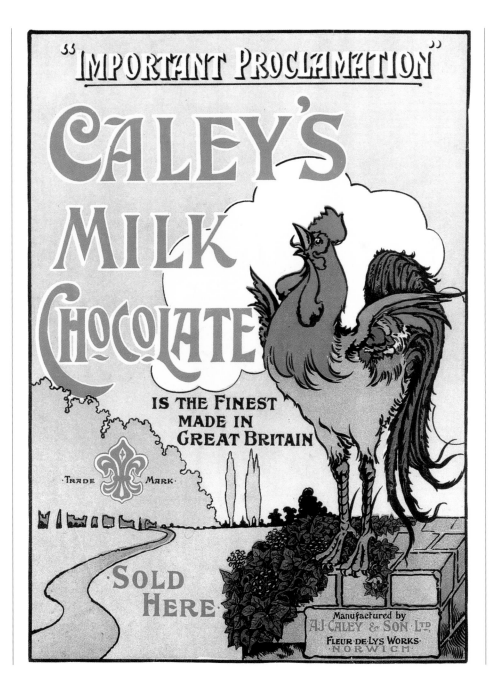

ABOVE *Confectionery range of the mid-1900s. By this time all the main chocolate firms were producing milk chocolate bars, and the popular lines, such as chocolate cremes or drops, could be purchased loose by weight or (more expensively) in a presentation card box. Chocolate tins were made for export or for special events; Rowntree's made a special tin for their delicacy, Swiss Milk Chocolate Croquetts.*

OPPOSITE *Fry's showcard c.1905. As ever, in the story of confectionery, a little bit of underhand temptation.*

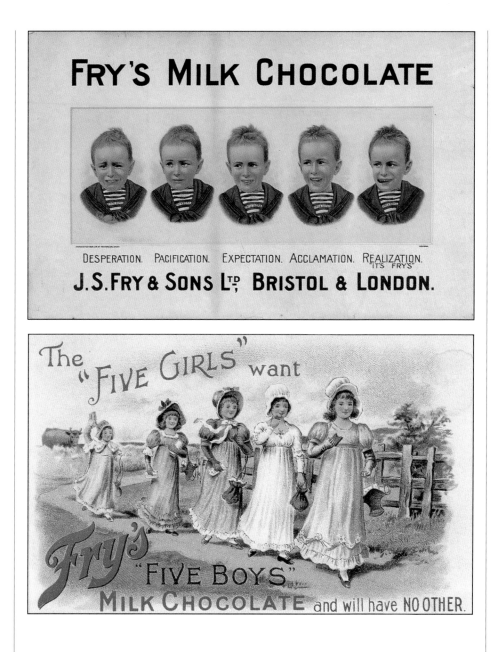

ABOVE *Fry's leaflet c. 1905, probably reduced down from a larger advertisement. Manufacturers often tempted their customers with the idea that milk chocolate or toffee was as sweet, or sweeter, than honey.*

OPPOSITE ABOVE *The classic Fry's advertisement created in 1886 to publicize all Fry's chocolate at the time. When the boy's face was photographed, a little ammonia had to be sprinkled in front of him to create the tearful look of 'desperation'.*

OPPOSITE BELOW *Fry's advertisement, c. 1905. Fry's obviously felt that 'five girls' were needed to accompany the 'Five Boys' (as this chocolate bar was now becoming known).*

ABOVE AND OPPOSITE *Fry's postcards, c. 1905.*
*Postcards were a popular form of
communication and were avidly collected.
Manufacturers often issued postcards which
were miniature versions of their showcard
advertisements; they proved sufficiently
popular for postcard companies to issue series
of showcard replicas. Fry's made sure that
their advertising portrayed every type of
child, from the guttersnipe to the Etonian.
(Above top left: illustration by John Hassall.
Above top right: illustration by Chas Pears.)*

ABOVE Packaging for toffee and chocolate
that contained Bovril, Oxo, Vitamalt or
Horlick's, 1900–35.

OPPOSITE Bovril poster illustrated by John
Hassall, 1902. Bovril Chocolate was
described as containing 'three hundred per
cent more actual nourishment than any other
Chocolate extant', and was recommended for
children and invalids, and specially suitable
for cyclists, sportsmen and travellers: 'a food
by the way.' Toffees with extra sustenance
were 'Just right for the children' (Boots), or
'A stand-by between meals' (Oxo).

ABOVE *Epps' advertising postcard, c. 1910. The message on this card must have been more than a little fanciful, since James Epps & Co never made much headway into the chocolate market; they were mainly noted for their homoeopathic cocoa, established in the 1850s.*
OPPOSITE *Stewart & Young showcard, c. 1910.*

ABOVE *Boisselier's showcard, c. 1910.*

OPPOSITE *Pascall's leaflet, c. 1915. This image
would have been used on posters, and the
girl's face was used to decorate one of
Pascall's tins.*

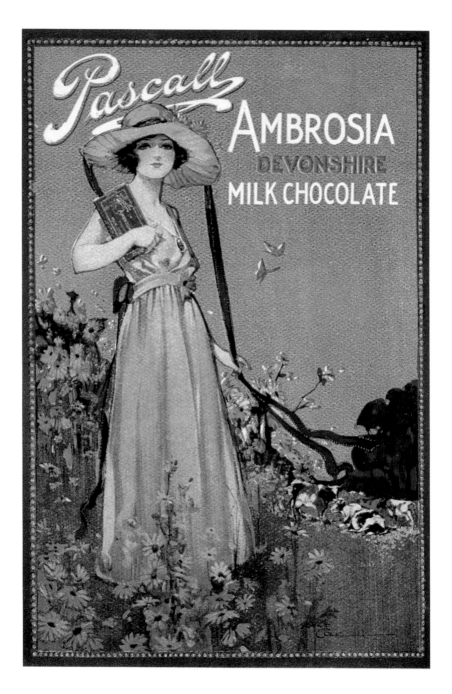

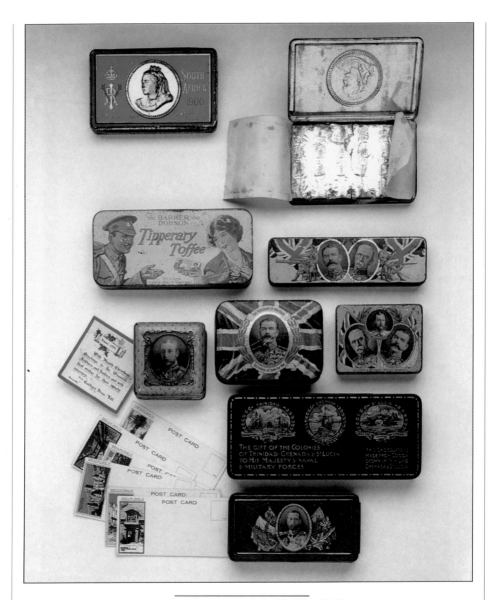

ABOVE *Confectionery tins commemorating the First World War, 1914–18, or sent to the troops containing chocolate. The Rowntree postcards were in a compartment at the base of the tin sent out for Christmas 1914.*

TOP *Queen Victoria's gift to the troops fighting in the Boer War, 1900. This unprecedented gesture meant that many of the 120,000 tins produced were kept – some still containing the ½lb slab of vanilla chocolate. Fry's, Cadbury's and Rowntree's split the order between them.*

Confectionery cigarette and cigar packets, 1900–35. Dunn's chocolate
cigarettes were sold in tins around 1900. During the First World War Fry's issued a
series of packets which featured the heroes of the moment (left to right: General
Smith-Dobrien, General Joffre). The heroes of the 1960s packets can be seen on
p. 104. By the 1930s sweet cigarette packets were imitating their life-size
counterparts.

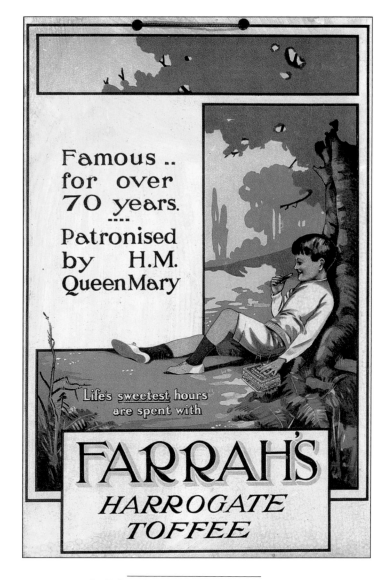

Famous ..
for over
70 years.

Patronised
by H.M.
Queen Mary

Life's sweetest hours
are spent with

FARRAH'S
HARROGATE
TOFFEE

ABOVE *Farrah's showcard, c.1915. Founded in 1840, Harrogate Toffee is still sold today in a tin of similar appearance to the original blue and silver design.*

OPPOSITE *Jackson & Smith's showcard, c.1915. Schoolboys, whether in or out of class, have always had an association with sweets.*

ABOVE *Meltis advertisement, c.1925, and a page from a 1922 trade catalogue, showing where an alteration was required to 'delete gold foil'. The factory at Bedford was built in 1913, especially for the manufacture of chocolate confectionery by Peek, Frean & Co, the biscuit company. In 1923 Meltis Limited was registered. Their most noted brand has been New Berry Fruits.*

OPPOSITE *Co-operative Wholesale Society toffee tin, c.1925. The co-operative societies were the largest retailers of consumer goods during the first half of this century. Confectionery was first produced by the CWS in 1873 at Crumpsall, Manchester, where biscuits had also just begun to be baked.*

ABOVE *Caley's and Mackintosh's confectionery tins, early 1920s. Rag Time was still the fashionable tempo, soon to be followed by the Jazz era. Mackintosh's caught the mood of the moment by their clever phrase 'everybody's chewing it', an adaption of Irving Berlin's hit title 'Everybody's Doin' It'.*
OPPOSITE *Kinema confectionery tins, early 1920s. The influence of the cinema was also imported from the United States. The two most popular film stars at the time, Mary Pickford and Charlie Chaplin, are depicted on these tins, though Pickford's likeness is not good and she had lost her curls with the new 'bobbed' hair style. Chaplin made a triumphant return to Britain in 1921, at the height of his popularity.*

ABOVE *Parkinson's shaped showcard, c. 1925.*
The image nicely reflects the slogan, 'too full
for words'.
OPPOSITE *Fry's shaped showcard, c. 1925. The*
traditional shape of the milk-churn was often
used to indicate dairy goodness.

ABOVE *Toffee tins, 1915–30. There have been
hundreds of toffee manufacturers in Britain,
including Lovell's of Newport, founded in
1884 and famed for their Toffee Rex ('the
king of toffees'), Thorne's, makers of Health
Cocoa, who claimed to make 'the world's
premier toffee', and Murray's of London who
were the first to make caramels in Britain.*

OPPOSITE *Walters' Palm Toffee tins, c. 1925.
Established in 1887, they were at one time a
large toffee producer crediting themselves
with 'the most delicious of all toffees'.
Walters conceived the recipe for Palm Toffee
in 1922. The toffee slab here is, in fact, for
display, and is made of plaster.*

ABOVE and OPPOSITE *Sharp's toffee tins with Sir Kreemy Knut and the trade mark parrot 'Always on top of the poll'. Edward Sharp ran a grocery business in the 1870s and 1880s, also making confectionery for the local area. In 1889 the first professional sugar boilers were installed. Kreemy Toffee was introduced in 1911 and the next year Supreem. It was around 1915 that the Macaw parrot trade mark was used along with the slogan 'Sharp's Toffee speaks for itself'. In 1919 Super Kreem was established with a new recipe, and Smith's Advertising Agency engaged. The result was Sir Kreemy Knut, and the advertising campaign of the next three years dramatically increased sales. Not only did Sir Kreemy Knut become the best-known salesman in Britain, but Sharp's became the world's largest toffee manufacturer. Sharp's were taken over by Trebor in 1961.*

ABOVE and OPPOSITE *Shaped posters for Rowntree's Pastilles and Clear Gums,*
c. 1925. These posters were sometimes attached behind the glass of the shop window
rather than at the back of the window display or behind the counter.

OVERLEAF *Traveller's sample case of the late 1920s, containing 48 varieties of*
Marsh's boiled sweets including Arctic Mints, West Indian Limes, Banana Bon-
Bons, Chocolate Satins, Old Tyme Winter Drops, Children's Hour Mixture and
Granny's Mint Lollies. The sweets on the left hand side are wrapped in Cellophane,
a revolutionary clear film introduced in the late 1920s which eventually replaced
paper sweet wrappers. The case is constructed in the solid style of the 1920s, and
with contents weighs 20 lbs.

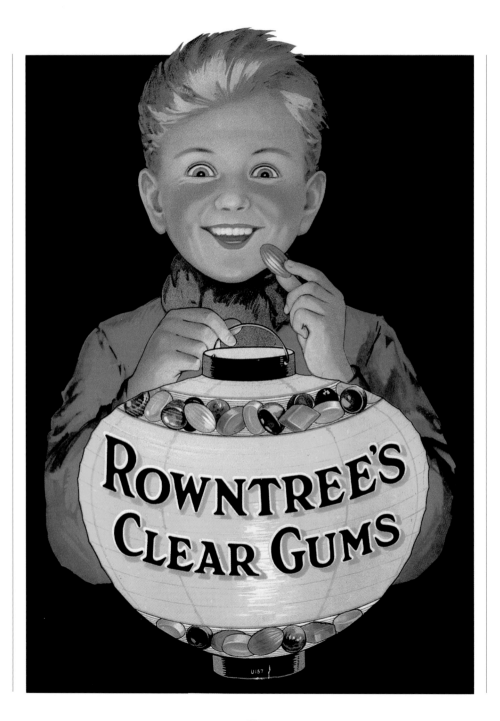

ABOVE *Cadbury's Milk Tray boxes, late 1920s*
and 1930s. Tray Chocolates were available
loose from 1914 (and Milk from 1915). Both
varieties were also sold in boxes from 1916,
the ¼lb and ½lb sizes claiming to be 'The
box for the pocket'.

OPPOSITE *Cadbury's 'tastes that thrill' poster,*
1927. Cadbury's boy showcard, c.1930.
Cadbury's sixteen-sheet poster 'eat more
milk', the glass and a half campaign that
started in 1928.

ABOVE *A selection of confectionery available at the end of the 1920s. J. Lyons & Co
opened their first tea shop in 1894; they started to make chocolates from 1909 and
other confections followed, including Kiskandies made under the Maison Lyons
name (reserved for better-class products). Cadbury's Mayfair Chocolates were
launched in 1928. Apart from Rowntree's Motoring Chocolate (launched 1926),
the glove compartment might also carry a tin of Smith Kendon's Mixed Fruit
Tablets containing glucose.*
OPPOSITE *Caley's poster, late 1920s. This slip-of-a-girl in party mood seems to be
unsure as to whether she should or should not eat the chocolate.*

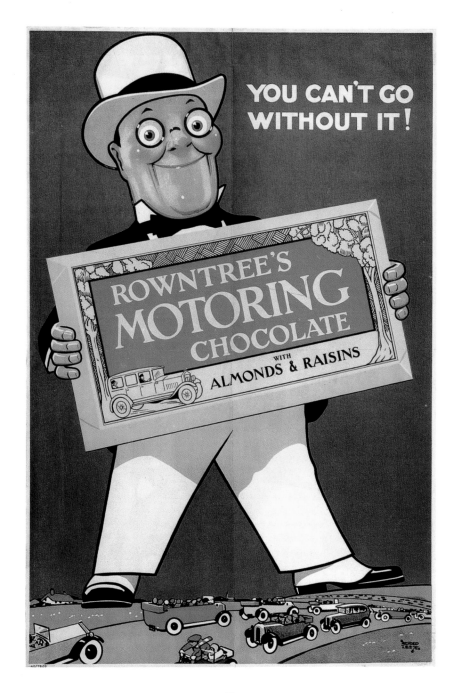

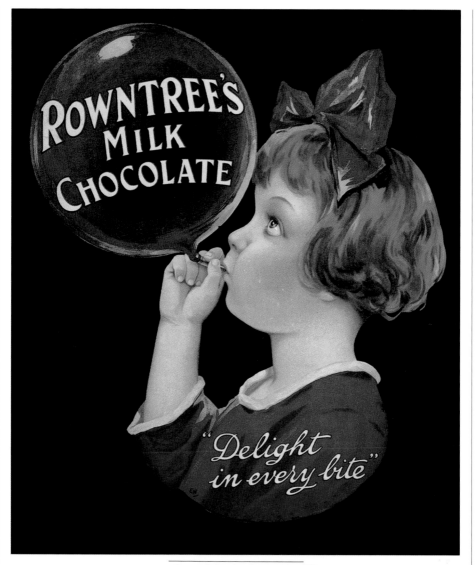

ABOVE *Rowntree's shaped window poster, late 1920s.*

OPPOSITE *Rowntree's poster, 1928. The character holding the bar of chocolate is Mr York, drawn by Alfred Leete and used by Rowntree's as a front man; visitors to the factory works not only received a presentation box of chocolates, but also a booklet called 'A Talk and a Walk with Mr York'. Introduced in 1926, Motoring Chocolate also came in 'milk' with the sustaining almonds and raisins (blue wrapper). Motoring Chocolate was withdrawn in 1964.*

ABOVE *Toffee tins using popular characters, 1920s and 1930s. Jackie Coogan's Toffee from S. Rogers & Co arrived within a few years of the child star's success in the film The Kid (1921). Felix Toffee from R.K. Confectionery was around at the same time. The cartoon character of Felix the Cat was born in 1919 and published as a cartoon strip in Britain by 1923 in Pearson's Weekly. Parker's Tiger Tim Toffee probably came out around 1930; special permission had been sought from Tiger Tim's Weekly (1920-40). Tiger Tim was originally created for a comic strip in the Daily Mirror of 1904. Mickey Mouse Toffee was launched in 1934 by Sharp's who took the whole of the front of the Daily Mail for 25 August in that year. Of all the merchandizing characters, Mickey Mouse has been the most successful.*

OPPOSITE *Edmondson's Cruising Toffees Tin, early 1930s, in the shape and colours of a Cunard liner's funnel.*

Christmas time is "Carnival" time —

Mackintosh's
TOFFEE DE LUXE

ABOVE *Mackintosh advertisement, 1929, illustrated by Jean d'Ylen.*
OPPOSITE *Mackintosh display card, c. 1930. Carnival Assortment was a popular Christmas gift of toffee varieties available from 1925, but it could not survive the excitement of Quality Street which Mackintosh's launched in 1936.*

ABOVE *Fox's display card, early 1930s. The Leicester wholesale grocery business of Joyce and Fox was extended to sweet manufacture in the 1890s, but in 1897 the partnership was dissolved. W.R. Fox continued to make sweets, and was joined in 1914 by his son, Eric, who had returned from studying business methods in America. In 1919 the firm registered the name Glacier, and the manufacturing business became known as Fox's Glacier Mints from 1925. Vigorous advertising during the early 1920s established the Mints nationally along with the polar bear character.*

OPPOSITE *Bassett's display tin, late 1920s and display cards, c. 1950. Liquorice All-Sorts came about by chance in 1899. A sample tray of liquorice lines was inadvertently knocked to the floor in front of a wholesaler; the resulting mixture of sweets looked so exciting that the wholesaler asked for a supply of all sorts to be mixed up together. The character of Bertie Bassett first appeared in the late 1920s.*

ABOVE *Terry's products, including boxed bars of chocolate, c. 1935, and a trade catalogue of 1937 showing Terry's Chocolate Orange (launched 1932) and Chocolate Apple. Terry's Snack contained raisins and 'nutritive' cereal, aimed at those joining the craze for hiking.*
OPPOSITE *Terry's display card, c. 1930. Theobroma chocolates were packed in a box made to look like a book. In 1735 the famous botanist, Linaeus, had named the cacao tree Theobroma cacao meaning 'the food of the gods'.*

ABOVE and OPPOSITE *Blue Bird showcards,
c. 1935. In 1895 Harry Vincent set up as a
sugar confectioner near Birmingham with the
ambition to build a factory in the country
which would not only be very beautiful but
also a pleasant place to work. He realised his
ambition in 1927 when his factory 'mid
pastures green' was built, and a special tin
was produced with the factory on the lid. Up
till this time the toffee was called Harvino,
but when Harry Vincent came across
Maeterlink's play The Blue Bird of Happiness
he renamed it Blue Bird.*

ABOVE *Fry's display cards, c.1935. Crunchie was launched in 1929 and wrapped in a distinguished looking embossed gold foil. In the 1940s this became an orange paper wrapper. In the 1960s Crunchie was wrapped in a foiled paper film, replaced in the late 1970s by a new type of gold foil.*

OPPOSITE *Quality Street display card with dummy sweets, 1937. Mackintosh's launched Quality Street in 1936. It was a mixture of eighteen different sweets and sold for 6d a ¼lb. The promotional literature for the trade announced 'the greatest advance yet made of any assortment'. A 'Handy' Cellophane packet at 6d was available, along with the standard tins and boxes.*

ABOVE and OPPOSITE *Fry's and Cadbury's advertisements mounted on wooden boards, late 1930s. Showing the standard range of 'countline' products, these advertisements were for long-term use. Indeed, the one for Cadbury's was still in use during the 1950s, the prices having been updated by hand.*

caught me under the mistletoe! I was just about to give the wretch a piece of my mind when he whipped out a box of Black Magic. So what could I do? Those chocs would soften the hardest heart

7/6 Casket (2⅛ lb... as illustrated)
(THREE LAYERS) No. 290.

5/- Casket (1¼ lb... as illustrated)
(THREE LAYERS) No. 291.

(53)

3/- Casket (1 lb... as illustrated but without ribbon)
(TWO LAYERS) No. 292.

Black Magic advertisement in a trade catalogue for 1939. In the early 1930s extensive market research was undertaken to find the ideal formula for a box of chocolates. Some 7000 consumers and 2000 retailers were interviewed; people expressed a preference for a quality chocolate without excessive packaging. It was also found that 60 per cent of boxed chocolates purchased by men were then presented to women. Of the hundreds of dark chocolate centres tested, twelve were selected (and they still remain the same today). Black Magic was launched in 1933 at 2/10d a pound. Soon after the 'letter' campaign (as above and page 95) was introduced; it ran at intervals until the final burst in 1974. The classic black and white box stayed the same until 1971.

Confectionery from the late 1930s. Of all the decades, the 1930s saw the birth of more world-beating confectionery brands than any other: Black Magic – largest plain chocolate assortment; Mars Bars – greatest value of any confectionery line; Kit Kat – enough produced to top the Empire State Building over four times every hour. Other notable launches were Maltesers, Smarties, Rolo, Roses and Dairy Box (the first time that the individual varieties were depicted with their description on the outside of the box). At this time the firm of Robertson & Woodcock (founded in 1907) launched a number of lines including their Trebor Mints in 1935 and Refreshers soon after.

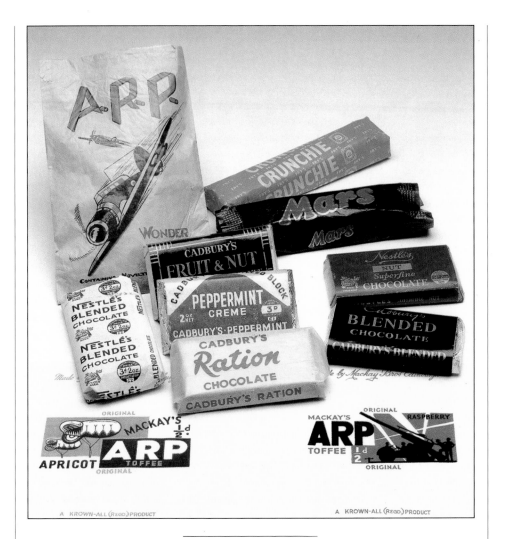

ABOVE *Sweets from the 1940s. Images of the Second World War were depicted on more ephemeral packs than the durable tins of the First World War. For instance, Mackay's Toffee illustrated anti-aircraft guns, barrage balloons and search lights; the A.R.P. (Air Raid Precautions) Wonder Bag showed fighter 'planes. Rationing (from 1942) introduced an allocation of points to everyone, restricting sweet consumption to 3oz per head per week. Wrappers indicated the controlled price and category into which a product fell. Cadbury's even issued a brand called Ration Chocolate. The lack of full-cream milk meant that separated milk was used, the result being termed 'blended chocolate'.*

OPPOSITE *Magazine advertisement, June 1953, celebrates the coronation of Queen Elizabeth II, and the final lifting of sweet rationing (February 1953). In fact, for a few months in 1949 rationing had been lifted for children (causing some resentment amongst the adults).*

ABOVE *Fry's magazine advertisement,
1952. Punch was a new bar containing the
three most popular confectionery tastes –
chocolate, caramel and fudge. A winning
combination that apparently won the girl at
the cost of 4d and two points from the ration
book. (Fry's had already tried out a bar called
Judy – see page 87.)*

OPPOSITE *Murray's magazine advertisement,
1955. An image from the Murraymint
cartoon TV advertisement transmitted
during the first commercial break on 22
September 1955.*

"THAT MAN THERE!"
"I'M FINISHING MY MURRAYMINT!"
Murraymints
the too-good-to-hurry mints
Suck a delicious MURRAYMINT flavoured (ever so discreetly) with a hint of mint. MURRAYMINTS have a taste you never tire of. They're mellow, refreshing and very long lasting. Everybody loves MURRAYMINTS so always keep some handy.
-with a delicious hint of mint!

ABOVE and OPPOSITE *Magazine
advertisements, 1953–57.*

ABOVE *Magazine advertisements, 1954–57. The public were so hungry for sweets after the end of rationing that there was little need for advertising, until supplies of raw materials caught up with demand towards the end of 1955. Confectionery sales reached 8oz a week per head compared to 7oz before the war and 6½oz today. Bounty Bar was launched by Mars in 1951 and in 1956 they produced a plain variety.*

OPPOSITE *Rowntree's advertisement, 1956. Fruit Gums from a tube are flat, but those from a box are fruit-shaped.*

ABOVE *Fry's Tuck Shop display card, c.1955.*
RIGHT *Crunch advertisement, 1956.*
OPPOSITE *Spangles magazine advertisements,
1956–57. Mars introduced Spangles in 1948;
during the 1950s and 1960s it became one of
the swinging brands but it was withdrawn in
1984.*

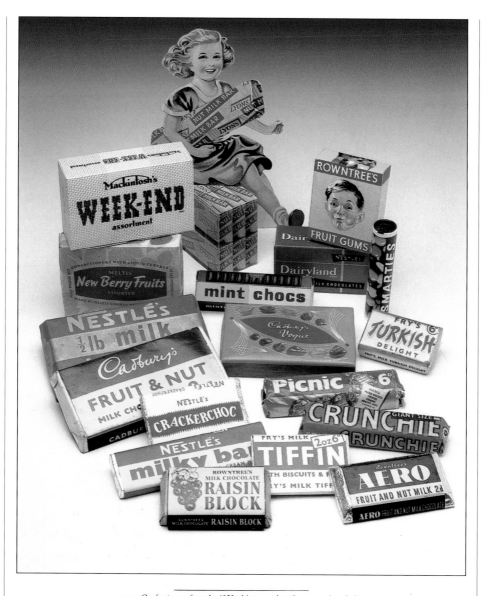

ABOVE *Confectionery from the 1950s. Many new brands were tried, including Nestlé's Dairyland, Fry's Picnic and Mackintosh's Week-End. In 1958 Smarties first used a plastic end for their tubes, later incorporating a single moulded letter of the alphabet.*
OPPOSITE *Cadbury's magazine advertisement, 1961, photographed at Piccadilly Circus in the heart of London.*

When
London
belongs
to you...

Make the day with Cadburys Milk Tray

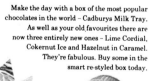

Make the day with a box of the most popular
chocolates in the world – Cadburys Milk Tray.
As well as your old favourites there are
now three entirely new ones – Lime Cordial,
Cokernut Ice and Hazelnut in Caramel.
They're fabulous. Buy some in the
smart re-styled box today.

¼ lb **1/7**   ½ lb **3/-**   1 lb **5/9**

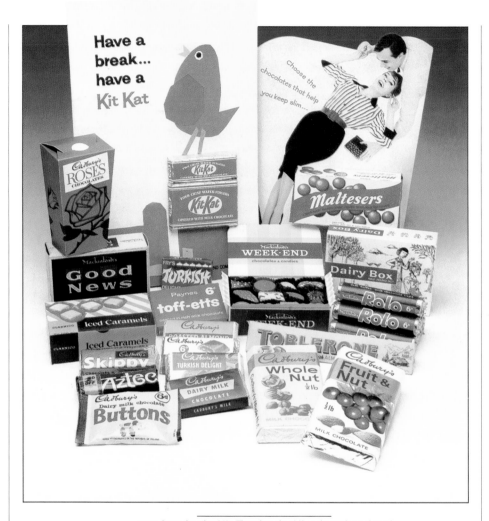

ABOVE *Sweets from the 1960s. Throughout the 1960s packaging design changed radically. For a time, around 1965, a number of drawings by the artist Peynet were adopted for Dairy Box. As ever, new brands continued to arrive: Good News, Aztec (a competitor of Mars Bar) and Skippy – not all survived. The slogan 'Have a break . . . Have a Kit Kat' was used from the time of Kit Kat's first TV commercial in 1957.*

OPPOSITE *Rowntree's display card, 1965. The After Eight range was launched in 1962; the wafer-thin mints struck the right tone and within a few years the rest of the range was dropped. During the 1960s sweet-shop window displays were at their most effusive, yet they disappeared fairly quickly in favour of the 'see-in' self-service confectioners. As a result the need for quantities of display material and dummy packs declined dramatically. The After Eight chocolates are dummies made from plaster. This was also the end of the era when each chocolate had an individual paper doily.*

ABOVE *Character Easter eggs, 1988. An interesting phenomenon of recent years has been the extraordinary increase in the range of chocolate Easter eggs, the ingenuity of their packaging and the number that are now tied with a television, film or book character. In 1988 there were Ghostbusters, Henry the Cat, Tom and Jerry, Mr Men, Danger Mouse, Thundercats, Rupert the Bear, EastEnders, Postman Pat, The Flintstones, Donald Duck and Roland Rat. One company that specialises in this field is Kinnerton (founded in 1978) who have produced eggs featuring Paddington Bear, Beatrix Potter, My Little Pony, Garfield, Thomas the Tank Engine, Fireman Sam, The Shoe People, Care Bears and Snoopy. In 1987 some £115 million was spent on hollow eggs.*

OPPOSITE *Sweet cigarette packets, late 1950s to 1979. In the 1950s sweet cigarette packets mainly imitated their adult counterparts. With the increasing influence of children's television programmes, firms began to link their products with the heroes of the small screen, such as Lenny the Lion and Andy Pandy. By the end of the 1970s the climate of opinion on smoking resulted in general agreement that the description 'sweet cigarettes' should be changed. 'Candy sticks' was the new name and by 1981 even some adults were sorry to see the familiar pink end disappear.*

THE MANUFACTURERS

Once upon a time sweets were made on a small scale, each area was served by the entrepreneurial activities of the local confectioner, and each confectioner built up his or her reputation for their own sticky delights. William Smith manufactured his glucose confectionery in small batches using copper pans over an open fire. He started in 1780 near Cheapside, London; the business became Smith Kendon. Mr Packer left Fry's in 1881 to start his company. He used a private house where he employed three people, a gas stove and several saucepans.

Each locality also had its favourite sweet – some still survive today. In the north there were Hawick Balls, Berwick Cockles, Jethart Snails and Galashiels Soor-Plooms. In Reading the local confectioner was proud of his 'celebrated Herbal Candy' which, according to his paper bags, had gained a 'marvellous reputation'.

Many of the early cocoa firms were started by Quakers or non-conformists, whose righteous upbringing and clean living made them good businessmen, preferring cocoa to alcohol. Fry, Cadbury, Rowntree, Terry and Mackintosh were all such men.

A number of companies became involved in confectionery by accident. One such was J. Lyons.

Something decorative was required for the windows of the first Corner House, which was opened in 1909. Chocolates were made on the premises and proved to be so popular that the business extended to the other teashops. In some cases, manufacturers known for totally different foods have dabbled in confectionery – the ice cream makers, Wall's, the biscuit manufacturer, Carr's, and the food preserver, Sharwood's, all sold toffee at some time.

Small firms making small quantities for small areas was how the confectionery industry started, but then came mechanization and the possibility of wider distribution. National advertising became a reality to those who could afford it. The result was the survival of the fittest. During the late nineteenth century and early twentieth, people with foresight, courage and ability geared themselves to the production of quality goods, selling them in greater and greater quantities. A more detailed look at the development of the larger manufacturing companies follows.

BELOW *Confectionery tin showing John Gray's factory in Glasgow, c. 1895.*
OPPOSITE *Fry's poster, c. 1880.*

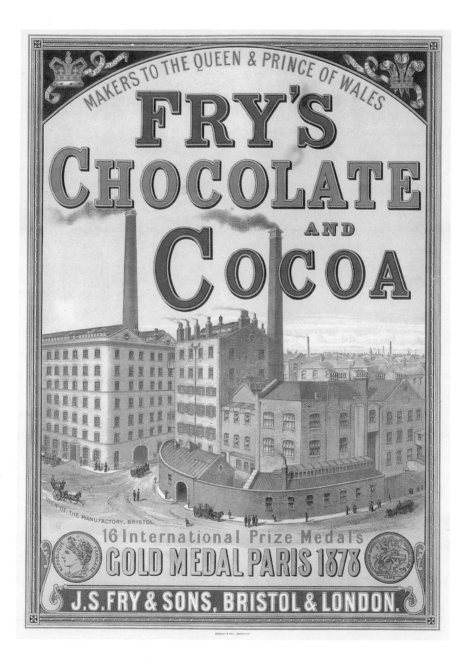

FRY

The firm of J.S. Fry & Sons is one of the oldest chocolate manufacturers in the country, going back to 1728 when Walter Churchman owned a shop in Small Street, Bristol. In the following year he was granted Letters Patent by George II enabling him to manufacture drinking chocolate. It is recorded that this patent was bought from him in 1761 by a Quaker physician called Doctor Joseph Fry (1728-1787). However, an advertisement in a local Bristol newspaper six years prior to this date, announced 'the best sorts of chocolate, made and sold wholesale and retail by Joseph Fry, Apothecary, in Small Street, Bristol'.

Later, trading under the name of Fry, Vaughan and Company, the business moved to Wine Street, before settling in Union Street, a fashionable part of town, in 1771. During this period cocoa was an expensive commodity (due to excessive import

The first pack of 1902, priced 6d, and the last of 1971, priced 7d.

duties) and was available only to the wealthy, so it was important that the shop was located in an up-market area. On Joseph's death the firm was managed by his wife Anna and his son Joseph Storrs Fry, after whom the company is now known. In 1795 the firm received a patent from George III allowing them to install a new type of roasting machine, shortly followed by the introduction of a Watt's steam engine to drive it.

It was under Joseph Storrs' son, Francis, and his nephew (also called Joseph Storrs) that the company rapidly expanded. One reason behind this growth was the firm's decision to step up production of eating chocolate, in particular the introduction of Fry's Cream Sticks in 1853, known from 1866 as Chocolate Cream Bars. Further success was afforded to the company by the introduction of Fry's Milk Chocolate in 1902, later to be known as Fry's Five Boys.

Early sponsorship from the firm included funding towards Captain Scott's expedition to Antarctica in 1910. In a letter of endorsement, Captain Scott stated 'Messrs. J.S. Fry and Sons supplied our Cocoa, sledging and fancy Chocolate, delicious comforts excellently packed and always in good condition . . . Crunching those elaborate chocolates brought one nearer to civilization than anything we experienced sledging.'

In 1919 Fry's and Cadbury's merged into one parent company, but the Fry's name is still in evidence today. Other products for which Fry's is known include Turkish Delight (introduced in 1914), Crunchie (1929), Tiffin (1937) and Picnic (1958).

Fry's products were taken by Captain Scott on his British Antarctic Expedition to the South Pole in 1910.

CADBURY

The Cadbury's story is an intriguing study of over 150 years of social – as well as industrial – development. The firm began life at number 93 Bull Street, Birmingham, in 1824. It was the project of a young Quaker called John Cadbury who at the age of twenty-two persuaded his father to fund the business. At this time the shop sold mainly tea and coffee; any cocoa that was required was ground by hand in a pestle and mortar. John Cadbury was particularly attuned to the commercial benefits of marketing and promotion, and one of his early attention-grabbing gimmicks was the employment of a Chinaman in full native costume to serve behind the counter. In 1831 a small factory was rented in Crooked Lane in order to facilitate greater production, and by 1841 the firm is recorded as selling sixteen different varieties of drinking chocolate. Twelve years later the firm acquired the highly prestigious Royal Warrant as suppliers to Queen Victoria.

Such was the workload during this period in the firm's history that John called in his brother Benjamin to help him manage the business before finally handing over to his two sons, Richard and

Cadbury booklets, c.1930. The firm's Quaker origins gave rise to the desire for the industry to grow up in an 'atmosphere free from drabness and depression'.

George. The company's fortunes had undoubtedly declined and the two brothers had to work hard to get it back onto a sound financial footing. A factor behind the company's change of fortune was the development of cocoa essence. Having visited the Dutch firm of Van Houten, leaders in the field of cocoa production, the brothers instigated a new production process in 1866; cocoa butter was pressed out of the cocoa beans, producing the relatively pure cocoa essence. The cocoa butter that was left over was used to make a wide variety of eating chocolates, including chocolate cremes.

In 1879 the company had accrued sufficient funds to purchase 14½ acres of land outside Birmingham. Here they built a large new factory which they christened Bournville. (The name of Bournville was chosen because it was thought to sound French at a time when many of the best chocolates came from Europe.) After fifteen years George began his project to establish a village for the workers in the factory. Within seven years 313 houses were built and the Bournville Village Trust was established in 1900 to administer this new community. Houses in the village are as treasured today as they were when first built.

The new factory allowed the company to develop its range of products, and the employment in 1880 of a French master confectioner, Frederick Kinchelman, strengthened the company's interest in chocolate-covered assortments. These handmade confections were often packed in highly decorative boxes, some of them carrying paintings by Richard Cadbury.

Cadbury's Milk Chocolate – based on Swiss chocolate – was launched in 1897 and Cadbury's Dairy Milk followed in 1905. Five years later came the introduction of Bournville Plain Chocolate and, in 1915, Cadbury's Milk Tray. In the following years, Cadbury's launched Flake (1920), Fruit & Nut (1921), Brazil Nut (1925) and Whole Nut (1933). In 1919 the company merged with Fry's. Today the company produces a phenomenal quantity of confectionery: the Bournville site alone (one of many) produces 1500 tonnes of chocolate which is made into 1.6 million bars and other confectionery. Sophisticated new machinery allows them to produce 1100 Creme Eggs per minute and 1680 Wispa Bars in the same amount of time.

ROWNTREE

A woman by the name of Mary Tuke (at the age of thirty and as yet unmarried) opened a small grocer's shop in York; it was to prove the beginnings of a great empire. At first, the venture was illegal because she had not been granted the necessary licence by the York Merchant Adventurers Company. After a series of court hearings and subsequent fines she was eventually granted the rights in 1732 to trade as a grocer. Mary Tuke was joined in the business by her nephew, William Tuke, who gave his name to the company.

The manufacture of cocoa and chocolate is first mentioned on price lists dated 1785, when 'good chocolate' cost 2 shillings and 3 pennies, and cocoa 'nibs' cost 1 shilling and 10 pennies. By 1815 William Tuke and Sons included 'Chocolate manufacturer' at the top of their bills. By the time Henry Isaac Rowntree acquired the York business in 1862, it was manufacturing 12 cwts of cocoa a week.

Rowntree took over the York company intent on introducing new technology, and within two years he had acquired an old foundry in Tanner's Moat to replace the old Castlegate premises. He also started specializing in and promoting the more up-market 'Genuine Rock Cocoa'. Rock cocoa at this time was made up of a mixture of cocoa and sugar. Some

Pastilles box, c. 1930.

of the cheaper qualities included wheat substances, such as sago flour, to add bulk. In 1880 Rowntree's Elect Cocoa was introduced, based on a Dutch method of manufacture and using cocoa of the highest quality. At about this time the company was also manufacturing Chocolate Drops, Chocolate Beans, and Chocolate Balls costing 1d and ½d.

Traditionally, gum sweets were made mainly in France. However, H.I. Rowntree and Co (as they were now known) began to manufacture crystallized gums in 1881, these being the forerunners of

Label for counter display box, c. 1930.

today's Fruit Pastilles. Their success necessitated the purchase of additional premises, and in 1893-4 they began to produce 'clear gums', the ancestors of today's Fruit Gums.

One of the company's leading brands, Black Magic, was introduced in 1933, claiming to be 'the first chocolate assortment ever made to order for a mass market'. Extensive research was carried out prior to its launch, and the company took the unusual step of emphasizing the brand name at the expense of the company name.

Rowntree's today produce many other well-known confectionery brands including Kit Kat (launched in 1935 with the name Chocolate Crisp), Aero (1935), Dairy Box (1936), Smarties (1937), Polo Mints (1948), After Eight (1962) and Jellytots (1965). In 1969 Rowntree merged with John Mackintosh and in 1988 Rowntree Mackintosh was taken over by Nestlé.

MACKINTOSH

John Mackintosh founded his business in 1890 at the age of twenty-two. Together with his wife (of only a few days' standing) he opened a small pastry-cook shop in King Cross Lane, Halifax. The aim of the shop was to concentrate on only the best specialities including high-quality confectionery. To promote his shop Mackintosh blended a new toffee sold under the title 'Mackintosh's Celebrated

Showcard and tin, c. 1905.

The first Quality Street tin, 1936.

Toffee'. The secret of this highly successful confection was its blend of traditional English toffee (similar to a butterscotch) with the newly arrived caramel sweets from America. Mackintosh helped promote it by giving away free samples, a marketing practise less common then than it is now.

By 1903 the company had expanded and changed premises several times before it built its own factory in Queens Road, and acquired other existing factories within Halifax. The Queens Road factory was destroyed by fire in 1911 which necessitated the firm's move to its present location in the area around Halifax station. The Queens Road factory was rebuilt and it was here that chocolates were made, along with other products.

Toffee De Luxe was introduced during the first World War in 1917, and was available in a variety of flavours including chocolate-coated. Seven years later, the firm introduced Mackintosh Chocolate. However, with the acquisition of the Norwich-based firm of confectioners A.J. Caley & Son Ltd in 1932, a much wider range of chocolates was introduced. Caley's had been making chocolates since 1886, and their expertise contributed much to the success of Mackintosh.

Other confectionery brands that are manufactured by Mackintosh include Quality Street (launched in 1936), Rolo (1937), Week-End (1957), Munchies (1957), Caramac (1959), Good News (1960), Toffee Crisp (1963), Tooty Frooties (1963) and Reward (1965).

TERRY

Terry's is one of Britain's oldest confectionery-making companies. It can trace its roots back to 1767 when two men called Berry and Bayldon set up business in Bootham, York. The confectionery they produced at that time consisted largely of sugar sweets, lozenges, comfits and candied peel.

When Joseph Terry joined the company in 1828 and took control shortly afterwards, he brought with him an apothecary's training, invaluable in ensuring consistent standards of high quality. The firm moved to St Helen's Square, York, at about the same time, where a restoration of the original shop still exists. Other confections that the company produced in these early days were conversation lozenges bearing messages such as 'Can you polka?' and 'Love me'.

By the middle of the nineteenth century the company had firmly established its reputation, both at home and abroad, and to meet growing demand, it set up a new factory in 1862 at Clementhorpe, not far away. By this time, Joseph Terry had been succeeded by his son also called Joseph and later to be knighted by Queen Victoria.

Above all, Terry's is admired for its chocolate. It was one of the first confectionery companies to produce the novelty of eating – rather than drinking – chocolate. It built a factory entirely for the purpose of manufacturing chocolate and, in 1867, a price list included 'thirteen different kinds of choco-

Leaflet, c. 1895.

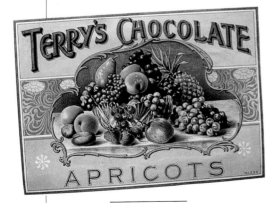

Label for counter display box, c. 1890.

late creams as well as batons, tablets and medallions. Seeing the market potential, the firm was also quick to introduce the idea of boxed assorted chocolates. Neopolitans were introduced as far back as 1899, and All Gold first appeared in 1932. One chocolate delight for which Terry's is perhaps best known is their Chocolate Orange, also introduced in 1932.

Miniature display card, c.1900.

NESTLÉ

Henri Nestlé was interested in products for children. His company started in 1866 at Vevey, Switzerland, where he marketed the first baby milk food. This was to develop into the now familiar Nestlé Condensed Milk and Ideal Milk.

By chance, Henri Nestlé's neighbour was a chocolate manufacturer called Daniel Peter. At some time they must have wondered what would happen if they combined their products and when Peter tried it, he found the result most palatable. The year was 1875 and Peter's Chocolate became the first commercial milk chocolate.

The Nestlé and Peter companies began to work closely together and in 1905 they produced a very sweet chocolate developed by the Nestlé company. It was at this time that Nestlé's chocolate began to be distributed widely in Britain, helped by the extensive use of vending machines prior to the First World War. The red cast-iron vending machines containing 1d chocolate bars became a common sight on the hundreds of railway stations around the country.

Nestlé's launched a wide variety of chocolate bars including probably the largest single bar; it weighed one pound and sold during the 1930s for 1/6d. In 1937 Milky Bar arrived, causing quite a sensation because the chocolate was white. It was thought especially suitable for children, being made with cocoa butter, milk and sugar. Today 100 million Milky Bars are sold a year.

Vending machine, c.1920.

BARKER & DOBSON

Barker & Dobson was founded in 1834 by a husband-and-wife team, Barker being his surname and Dobson being her maiden name. They established a small confectionery shop in Paradise Street, Liverpool, and their stock included the very best quality chocolates and confectionery, some makes having been imported especially from Europe.

However, it took nearly sixty years for the business to warrant being moved to larger premises in Hope Street in 1892. It was here that they began to make their own confectionery instead of selling other companies' products. The two men who were responsible for turning the business into an international concern were Henry Dobson Jacobson and Percy Jacobson, grandchildren of the founders. To ensure high quality they personally sampled sweets every morning right up until they died in 1961 aged 95 and 90, perhaps a testament to the healthy properties of the confections. Among other achievements, they were responsible for introducing the novelty of wrapping sweets individually. Under their leadership Buttered Brazils were a particularly successful range, and Creamy Mints were introduced in 1933. By 1939 they manufactured around 450 different varieties of confectionery.

Cachou jars, 1920s.

Since those days, the number of varieties has dropped but the tonnage has increased quite considerably. Barker & Dobson's brand leader is Everton Mints, although other popular brands include Princess Almonds, Glacé Mints, Nut Brittle, Barley Sugar, Chocolate Eclairs, Buttered Brazils and Chocolate Dragees.

Poster, c.1895.

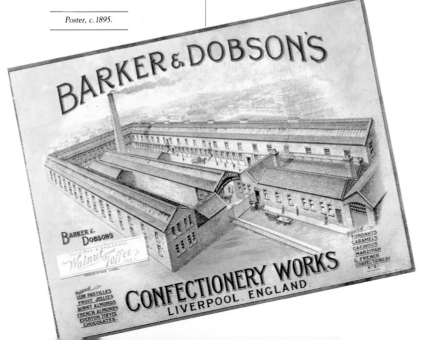

PASCALL

From its humble beginnings in a two-roomed shop off Oxford Street, London, over a hundred years ago, the firm of Pascall has established itself as a well-known name in the confectionery market. Its founder, James Pascall, was of Huguenot descent and began his career, first by working for his father in the bakery business, and then as an agent for Cadbury's. In 1866 he set up in business with his brother Alfred. Early sweets that they manufactured included herbal cough drops, candy and French rock, but when they moved to a larger premises in Valentine Place, Blackfriars, in 1877, they extended their range to include barley sugar, sugar sticks and almond rock. Their break into chocolate came in 1878 with the introduction of their 1d Berlin Chocolate Cremes.

A devastating fire swept through their premises in 1897. It was started by a former employee, a man of 'weak intellect' who confessed to arson and was dealt with leniently being given three years penal servitude. The fire precipitated the firm's move to their present location in Mitcham, Surrey. In the later years of the nineteenth century Pascall also imported and sold foreign goods, including confectionery from 'the best factory in Paris'. Naturally enough, such imports were not cheap: Molonides Argentees (silver melons), for example, cost a handsome three shillings for a 'parcel'.

Pascall's sweet tin, c. 1910.

Pascall is perhaps best known for its boiled sweets which, traditionally, were sold either from large glass jars on the confectioner's shelf or from tin canisters. Other confectionery for which they are known includes marshmallows. Along with Murray's, Pascall came under Beecham's umbrella briefly in the 1960s, but more recently were taken over by Cadbury's.

Pascall's Toffee box, c. 1920.

BASSETT

The firm of Bassett's has a history of over 140 years of sweet-making, going back to around 1842 when George Bassett founded the company. At that time, he is recorded in the Sheffield Directory of Traders as a 'wholesale confectioner, lozenge maker and British wine trader'. A particularly quirky incident for which George Bassett is remembered is the making of a giant cake. To celebrate the proclamation of peace with Russia in 1856, his firm baked a cake which, complete with icing, weighed 9767 lb; the cake was an early piece of brilliant publicity for the firm.

However, Bassett's is perhaps best known for its most successful seller over the last ninety years – Liquorice Allsorts, devised in 1899. The concept of marketing an assortment of liquorice shapes and creme-paste sweets owed less to the firm's deliberate policy than to the hand of chance. This happy accident is credited to a member of the Bassett's sales team called Charlie Thompson. The story goes that one day his boxes of so-called buttons, cubes and nuggets of liquorice and creme-paste sweets were inadvertently knocked on to the floor in front of a potential buyer. On seeing such an attractive mixture the buyer immediately instructed him to tell Bassett's to package an assortment, and the rest is history. As a measure of their gratitude, the company asked Charlie Thompson to name the new product and Liquorice Allsorts were born. Despite poor sales at the start, the company now produces over 14 million sweets a day, many of which are exported to Europe and the United States.

Trade card, c. 1930.

The company produces other liquorice products, most notably Pontefract cakes (sometimes known as Yorkshire pennies) which bear the seal of the region. Catherine wheels, pipes and bootlaces are among the playful shapes made particularly to appeal to children. Different types of sweets that the company manufactures – appealing to adults as much as to children – are wine gums, dolly mixtures and the rather peculiar but extremely successful jelly babies.

Through the years Bassett's have taken over a number of other companies, including the liquorice producers Voile & Wortley of London in 1956 and Wilkinson's of Pontefract in 1961. In 1966 Bassett's bought the firm of Barratt's, established in London since 1848 and the largest sugar confectionery manufacturer in the country employing 1300 people. Barratt's were the acknowledged leaders in the children's 'own purchase' market, producing an extensive range of 1d sweets such as the aptly named Red Hot Mint Balls and their famous Sherbet Fountains and Sherbet Sucker Dab ('the best value on earth').

CALLARD & BOWSER

The name of Callard & Bowser is perhaps most often associated with Cream-Line Toffees, a brand of confectionery which the company introduced in 1937. In fact, the company's history goes back over 150 years to 1837 when Daniel Callard and his brother-in-law, J. Bowser, set up a confectionery

Price card, c. 1935.

Nuttall's Mintoes and Thornton's Toffee tins, c. 1925.

and bakery business located in Finchley, London. In the late nineteenth century the firm moved to Euston and established machinery capable of producing Butterscotch and Dessert Nougat. Since then, the company has acquired several other companies, including William Nuttall of Doncaster (producers of Nuttall's Mintoes, introduced in 1909), Riley Brothers (the manufacturers of whipped cream Bon-Bons) and Smith Kendon (noted for their range of boiled sugar Travel Sweets).

THORNTON

Compared with many of the confectionery companies mentioned in this book, the firm of J.W. Thornton Ltd is a newcomer. It was founded in 1911 by Joseph William Thornton who opened a sweetshop in Sheffield, but it was his two sons, Norman and Stanley, who took the company into an era of commercial expansion. Originally sweets had been made in the cellar of the old shop, but in 1927 they bought a small factory. Among other countries, the firm looked to Switzerland to learn about the manufacture of confectionery. Today, they have established their reputation for quality 'handmade' chocolates and sweets, selling through their own chain of retail shops.

MARS

Today, more than two million Mars Bars are made each day in Britain alone. The firm of Mars Confectionery Ltd began life in 1932 in a small rented factory in Slough, Middlesex – a breakaway from the parent Mars company in the United States. At that time, most chocolate was sold in blocks, so the candy Mars Bars with their combination of nougat, caramel and chocolate were quite unusual. At first the bars were made by hand, but not for long. They

proved extremely popular and within the first year of business the workforce grew from twelve to a hundred.

It was Forrest Mars, the son of the American founder, who set up operation in Britain. He brought with him the recipe for the bars that were to become such a hit with the British public. Following the success of Mars Bars, he introduced Milky Way in 1935 (already launched in the United States by his father in 1923) and the following year Maltesers ('crisp malty centres covered with milky chocolate').

During the Second World War, Mars only produced their Bars. Then in 1948 Mars' first sugar confectionery brand was launched, Spangles. During the next twenty years a series of successful brands were developed – Bounty Bars (1951), Treets (1955), Galaxy (1958), Opal Fruits (1959), Topic (1962), and then in 1967 Twix, Revels and Marathon.

Magazine advertisement, 1946.

INDEX

ROWNTREE'S PASTILLES

CHOCOLATE MAKERS to H·M· the KING

"PLEASE EXCUSE MY BACK, BUT I'M BUSY!"

CHOCOLATE MAKERS to H·M· the KING

ACKNOWLEDGEMENTS

The illustrations for this book are the result of twenty-five years of searching for advertisements and packs, helped by friends and acquaintances throughout the country. Much of this material can now be seen at the Museum of Advertising and Packaging, Gloucester, where many other items from the Robert Opie Collection are on display.

For the background information I am most grateful to those confectionery manufacturers who provided details on their origins, namely: Barker & Dobson, Bassett, Cadbury, Callard & Bowser, Famous Names, Kinnerton, Lindt, Lovell, Lyons, Mars, Nestlé, Rowntree, Terry, Thornton, Tobler Suchard, Trebor, Wrigley. I would also like to thank the *Confectionery Manufacture and Marketing* magazine, Helge Rubinstein for writing *The Chocolate Book* (Macdonald, 1981), and Rayner Sharp for searching out his company's history. Finally my thanks go to Polly Powell for her invaluable assistance and encouragement during the moulding of this book.

Photographers: Paul Forrester, CPL, Robert Opie.

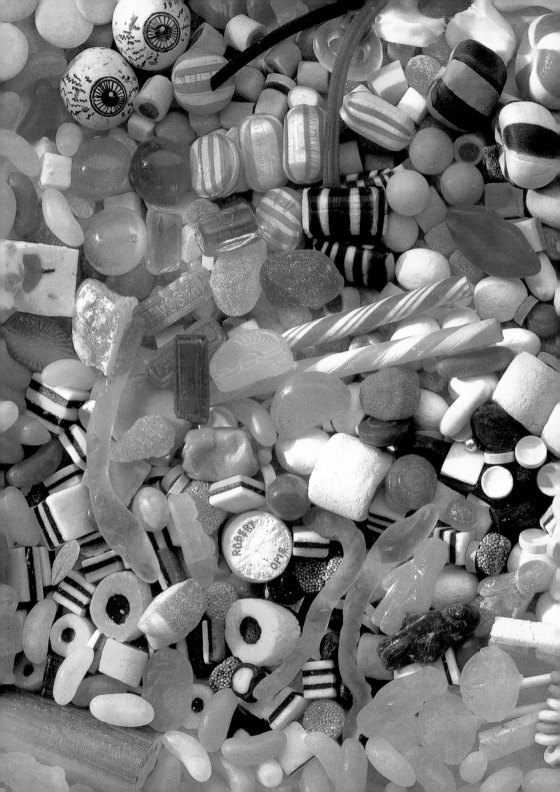

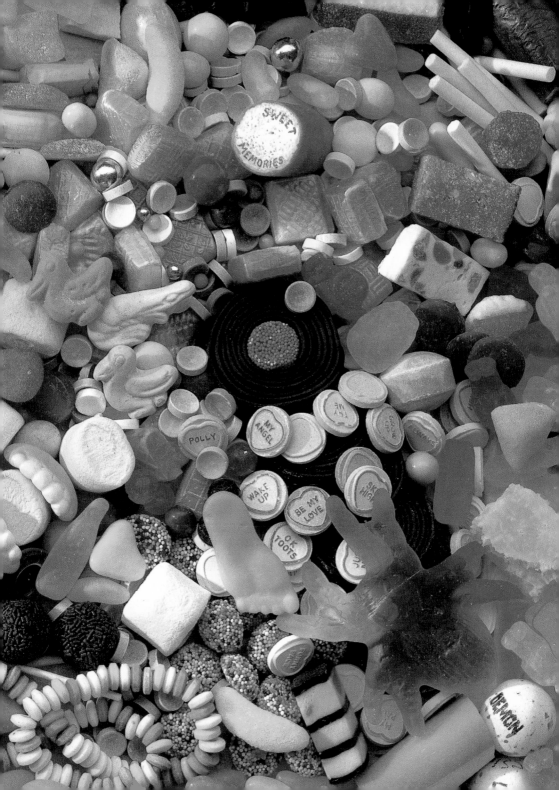